THE HISTORY & CULTURE
of NATIVE AMERICANS

The Choctaw

THE HISTORY & CULTURE of NATIVE AMERICANS

The Apache

The Blackfeet

The Cherokee

The Cheyenne

The Choctaw

The Comanche

The Hopi

The Iroquois

The Lakota Sioux

The Mohawk

The Nez Perce

The Navajo

The Seminole

The Zuni

THE HISTORY & CULTURE of NATIVE AMERICANS

The Choctaw

JOHN P. BOWES

Series Editor
PAUL C. ROSIER

CHELSEA HOUSE
PUBLISHERS
An imprint of Infobase Publishing

The Choctaw

Chelsea House
An imprint of Infobase Publishing
132 West 31st Street
New York NY 10001

Library of Congress Cataloging-in-Publication Data

Bowes, John P., 1973–
   The Choctaw / By John P. Bowes.
     p. cm. — (The history and culture of native Americans)
   Includes bibliographical references and index.
   ISBN 978-1-60413-788-0 (hardcover)
   1. Choctaw Indians—History—Juvenile literature. I. Title. II. Series.

   E99.C8B67 2010
   976.004'97387—dc22   2010011809

Chelsea House books are available at special discounts when purchased in bulk quantities for businesses, associations, institutions, or sales promotions. Please call our Special Sales Department in New York at (212) 967-8800 or (800) 322-8755.

You can find Chelsea House on the World Wide Web at
http://www.chelseahouse.com

Text design by Lina Farinella
Cover design by Alicia Post
Composition by Newgen
Cover printed by Bang Printing, Brainerd, MN
Book printed and bound by Bang Printing, Brainerd, MN
Date printed: September 2010
Printed in the United States of America

10 9 8 7 6 5 4 3 2 1
This book is printed on acid-free paper.

Contents

Foreword
by Paul C. Rosier

Native American words, phrases, and tribal names are embedded in the very geography of the United States—in the names of creeks, rivers, lakes, cities, and states, including Alabama, Connecticut, Iowa, Kansas, Illinois, Missouri, Oklahoma, and many others. Yet Native Americans remain the most misunderstood ethnic group in the United States. This is a result of limited coverage of Native American history in middle schools, high schools, and colleges; poor coverage of contemporary Native American issues in the news media; and stereotypes created by Hollywood movies, sporting events, and TV shows.

Two newspaper articles about American Indians caught my eye in recent months. Paired together, they provide us with a good introduction to the experiences of American Indians today: first, how they are stereotyped and turned into commodities; and second, how they see themselves being a part of the United States and of the wider world. (Note: I use the terms *Native Americans* and *American Indians* interchangeably; both terms are considered appropriate.)

In the first article, "Humorous Souvenirs to Some, Offensive Stereotypes to Others," written by Carol Berry in *Indian Country Today*, I read that tourist shops in Colorado were selling "souvenir" T-shirts portraying American Indians as drunks. "My Indian name is Runs with Beer," read one T-shirt offered in Denver. According to the article, the T-shirts are "the kind of stereotype-reinforcing products also seen in nearby Boulder, Estes Park, and likely other Colorado communities, whether as part of the tourism trade or as everyday merchandise." No other ethnic group in the United States is stereotyped in such a public fashion. In addition, Native people are used to sell a range of consumer goods, including the Jeep Cherokee, Red Man chewing tobacco, Land O'Lakes butter, and other items that either objectify or insult them, such as cigar store Indians. As importantly, non-Indians learn about American Indian history and culture through sports teams such as the Atlanta Braves, Cleveland Indians, Florida State Seminoles, or Washington Redskins, whose name many American Indians consider a racist insult; dictionaries define *redskin* as a "disparaging" or "offensive" term for American Indians. When fans in Atlanta do their "toma-hawk chant" at Braves baseball games, they perform two inappropri-ate and related acts: One, they perpetuate a stereotype of American Indians as violent; and two, they tell a historical narrative that covers up the violent ways that Georgians treated the Cherokee during the Removal period of the 1830s.

The second article, written by Melissa Pinion-Whitt of the San Bernardino *Sun* addressed an important but unknown dimension of Native American societies that runs counter to the irresponsible and violent image created by products and sporting events. The article, "San Manuels Donate $1.7 M for Aid to Haiti," described a Native American community that had sent aid to Haiti after it was devastated in January 2010 by an earthquake that killed more than 200,000 people, injured hundreds of thousands more, and destroyed the Haitian capital. The San Manuel Band of Mission Indians in California donated $1.7 million to help relief efforts in Haiti; San Manuel children held fund-raisers to collect additional donations. For the San Manuel Indians it was nothing new; in 2007 they had donated $1 million to help Sudanese refugees in Darfur. San Manuel also contributed $700,000 to relief efforts following Hurricane Katrina and Hurricane Rita, and donated $1 million in 2007 for wildfire recovery in Southern California.

Such generosity is consistent with many American Indian nations' cultural practices, such as the "give-away," in which wealthy tribal members give to the needy, and the "potlatch," a win-ter gift-giving ceremony and feast tradition shared by tribes in the

Pacific Northwest. And it is consistent with historical accounts of American Indians' generosity. For example, in 1847 Cherokee and Choctaw, who had recently survived their forced march on a "Trail of Tears" from their homelands in the American South to present-day Oklahoma, sent aid to Irish families after reading of the potato famine, which created a similar forced migration of Irish. A Cherokee newspaper editorial, quoted in Christine Kinealy's *The Great Irish Famine: Impact, Ideology, and Rebellion*, explained that the Cherokee "will be richly repaid by the consciousness of having done a good act, by the moral effect it will produce abroad." During and after World War II, nine Pueblo communities in New Mexico offered to donate food to the hungry in Europe, after Pueblo army veterans told stories of suffering they had witnessed while serving in the United States armed forces overseas. Considering themselves a part of the wider world, Native people have reached beyond their borders, despite their own material poverty, to help create a peaceful world community.

American Indian nations have demonstrated such generosity within the United States, especially in recent years. After the terrorist attacks of September 11, 2001, the Lakota Sioux in South Dakota offered police officers and emergency medical personnel to New York City to help with relief efforts; Indian nations across the country sent millions of dollars to help the victims of the attacks. As an editorial in the *Native American Times* newspaper explained on September 12, 2001, "American Indians love this country like no other. . . . Today, we are all New Yorkers."

Indeed, Native Americans have sacrificed their lives in defending the United States from its enemies in order to maintain their right to be both American and Indian. As the volumes in this series tell us, Native Americans patriotically served as soldiers (including as "code talkers") during World War I and World War II, as well as during the Korean War, the Vietnam War, and, after 9/11, the wars in Afghanistan and Iraq. Native soldiers, men and women, do so today by the tens of thousands because they believe in America, an

America that celebrates different cultures and peoples. Sgt. Leonard Gouge, a Muscogee Creek, explained it best in an article in *Cherokee News Path* in discussing his post-9/11 army service. He said he was willing to serve his country abroad because "by supporting the American way of life, I am preserving the Indian way of life."

This new Chelsea House series has two main goals. The first is to document the rich diversity of American Indian societies and the ways their cultural practices and traditions have evolved over time. The second goal is to provide the reader with coverage of the complex relationships that have developed between non-Indians and Indians over the past several hundred years. This history helps to explain why American Indians consider themselves both American and Indian and why they see preserving this identity as a strength of the American way of life, as evidence to the rest of the world that America is a champion of cultural diversity and religious freedom. By exploring Native Americans' cultural diversity and their contributions to the making of the United States, these volumes confront the stereotypes that paint all American Indians as the same and portray them as violent; as "drunks," as those Colorado T-shirts do; or as rich casino owners, as many news accounts do.

* * *

Each of the 14 volumes in this series is written by a scholar who shares my conviction that young adult readers are both fascinated by Native American history and culture and have not been provided with sufficient material to properly understand the diverse nature of this complex history and culture. The authors themselves represent a varied group that includes university teachers and professional writers, men and women, and Native and non-Native. To tell these fascinating stories, this talented group of scholars has examined an incredible variety of sources, both the primary sources that historical actors have created and the secondary sources that historians and anthropologists have written to make sense of the past.

Although the 14 Indian nations (also called tribes and communities) selected for this series have different histories and cultures, they all share certain common experiences. In particular, they had to face an American empire that spread westward in the eighteenth and nineteenth centuries, causing great trauma and change for all Native people in the process. Because each volume documents American Indians' experiences dealing with powerful non-Indian institutions and ideas, I outline below the major periods and features of federal Indian policy-making in order to provide a frame of reference for complex processes of change with which American Indians had to contend. These periods—Assimilation, Indian New Deal, Termination, Red Power, and Self-determination—and specific acts of legislation that define them—in particular the General Allotment Act, the Indian Reorganization Act, and the Indian Self-determination and Education Assistance Act—will appear in all the volumes, especially in the latter chapters.

In 1851, the commissioner of the federal Bureau of Indian Affairs (BIA) outlined a three-part program for subduing American Indians militarily and assimilating them into the United States: concentration, domestication, and incorporation. In the first phase, the federal government waged war with the American Indian nations of the American West in order to "concentrate" them on reservations, away from expanding settlements of white Americans and immigrants. Some American Indian nations experienced terrible violence in resisting federal troops and state militia; others submitted peacefully and accepted life on a reservation. During this phase, roughly from the 1850s to the 1880s, the U.S. government signed hundreds of treaties with defeated American Indian nations. These treaties "reserved" to these American Indian nations specific territory as well as the use of natural resources. And they provided funding for the next phase of "domestication."

During the domestication phase, roughly the 1870s to the early 1900s, federal officials sought to remake American Indians in the mold of white Americans. Through the Civilization Program, which actually started with President Thomas Jefferson, federal officials sent religious missionaries, farm instructors, and teachers to the newly created reservations in an effort to "kill the Indian to save the man," to use a phrase of that time. The ultimate goal was to extinguish American Indian cultural traditions and turn American Indians into Christian yeoman farmers. The most important piece of legislation in this period was the General Allotment Act (or Dawes Act), which mandated that American Indian nations sell much of their territory to white farmers and use the proceeds to farm on what was left of their homelands. The program was a failure, for the most part, because white farmers got much of the best arable land in the process. Another important part of the domestication agenda was the federal boarding school program, which required all American Indian children to attend schools to further their rejection of Indian ways and the adoption of non-Indian ways. The goal of federal reformers, in sum, was to incorporate (or assimilate) American Indians into American society as individual citizens and not as groups with special traditions and religious practices.

During the 1930s some federal officials came to believe that American Indians deserved the right to practice their own religion and sustain their identity as Indians, arguing that such diversity made America stronger. During the Indian New Deal period of the 1930s, BIA commissioner John Collier devised the Indian Reorganization Act (IRA), which passed in 1934, to give American Indian nations more power, not less. Not all American Indians supported the IRA, but most did. They were eager to improve their reservations, which suffered from tremendous poverty that resulted in large measure from federal policies such as the General Allotment Act.

Some federal officials opposed the IRA, however, and pushed for the assimilation of American Indians in a movement called Termination. The two main goals of Termination advocates, during the 1950s and 1960s, were to end (terminate) the federal reservation system and American Indians' political sovereignty derived from treaties and to relocate American Indians from rural reservations to urban areas. These coercive federal assimilation policies in turn generated resistance from Native Americans, including young activists who helped to create the so-called Red Power era of the 1960s and 1970s, which coincided with the African-American civil rights movement. This resistance led to the federal government's rejection of Termination policies in 1970. And in 1975 the U.S. Congress passed the Indian Self-determination and Education Assistance Act, which made it the government's policy to support American Indians' right to determine the future of their communities. Congress then passed legislation to help American Indian nations to improve reservation life; these acts strengthened American Indians' religious freedom, political sovereignty, and economic opportunity.

All American Indians, especially those in the western United States, were affected in some way by the various federal policies described above. But it is important to highlight the fact that each American Indian community responded in different ways to these pressures for change, both the detribalization policies of assimilation and the retribalization policies of self-determination. There is no one group of "Indians." American Indians were and still are a very diverse group. Some embraced the assimilation programs of the federal government and rejected the old traditions; others refused to adopt non-Indian customs or did so selectively, on their own terms. Most American Indians, as I noted above, maintain a dual identity of American and Indian.

Today, there are more than 550 American Indian (and Alaska Natives) nations recognized by the federal government. They have a legal and political status similar to states, but they have special rights and privileges that are the result of congressional acts and the hundreds of treaties that still govern federal-Indian relations today. In July 2008, the total population of American Indians (and Alaska Natives) was 4.9 million, representing about 1.6 percent of the United States population. The state with the highest number of American Indians is California, followed by Oklahoma, home to the Cherokee (the largest American Indian nation in terms of population), and then Arizona, home to the Navajo (the second-largest American Indian nation). All told, roughly half of the American Indian population lives in urban areas; the other half lives on reservations and in other rural parts of the country. Like all their fellow American citizens, American Indians pay federal taxes, obey federal laws, and vote in federal, state, and local elections; they also participate in the democratic processes of their American Indian nations, electing judges, politicians, and other civic officials.

This series on the history and culture of Native Americans celebrates their diversity and differences as well as the ways they have strengthened the broader community of America. Ronnie Lupe, the chairman of the White Mountain Apache government in Arizona, once addressed questions from non-Indians as to "why Indians serve the United States with such distinction and honor?" Lupe, a Korean War veteran, answered those questions during the Gulf War of 1991–1992, in which Native American soldiers served to protect the independence of the Kuwaiti people. He explained in "Chairman's Corner" in *The Fort Apache Scout* that "our loyalty to the United States goes beyond our need to defend our home and reservation lands. . . . Only a few in this country really understand that the indigenous people are a national treasure. Our values have the potential of creating the social, environmental, and spiritual healing that could make this country truly great."

—Paul C. Rosier
Associate Professor of History
Villanova University

Choctaw Emergence

"It takes a sacred space to heal a troubled spirit." Delores Love says these words to her family in the novel *Shell Shaker*, written by Choctaw author LeAnne Howe. This simple phrase explains why Love intends to bury a murdered chief near Nanih Waiya, a mound sacred to the Choctaw in Mississippi. Delores states that this burial is necessary to protect the living Choctaw from the return of a man who had done so much wrong in his life. They will take the chief's body and drive hundreds of miles from Oklahoma to Mississippi to make sure his spirit will not return to this world. Only Nanih Waiya, the Mother Mound, has that power.

Nanih Waiya is one of the grounding forces in *Shell Shaker*. The novel tells a story that weaves together the political, religious, and cultural lives of Choctaw men, women, and children in the mid-eighteenth and late twentieth centuries. It is a tale that uses the members of the Billy family to connect the Choctaw civil war of the 1740s to the divisive Choctaw politics of the 1990s in Oklahoma. In addition, *Shell Shaker* highlights critical elements of Choctaw identity, politics, history, and religion.

Although it is a work of fiction, *Shell Shaker* provides an excellent starting point for the following examination of Choctaw history. As a story written by a Choctaw woman about the experiences of the Choctaw people in the late twentieth century, it asserts the enduring presence of the Choctaw Nation and its culture. Just as important, Howe illustrates that the present cannot and should not be separated from the past. Events that are both centuries and decades old continue to reverberate in the culture and politics of the Choctaw living throughout the United States. It is at Nanih Waiya, then, that this history begins.

ORIGIN STORIES

Near the head of the Pearl River northeast of Philadelphia, Mississippi, there is a mound of earth that covers nearly three-quarters of an acre (0.3 hectares, or ha) of land. At some points, it is nearly 25 feet (7.62 meters, or m) high, and its base measures approximately 218 feet by 140 feet (66.4 by 42.7 m). The Choctaw call this earthen structure Nanih Waiya. This term has been translated as "the leaning mound," while some refer to it as "the Mother Mound." Although the mound does not lie in the exact center of what was once Choctaw territory in the late eighteenth century, it is a grounding force in Choctaw beliefs about their origins.

The importance of this sacred site is clearly illustrated in the bulletin written by an anthropologist named John R. Swanton and published by the Smithsonian Institution Bureau of American Ethnology in 1931. Swanton spent more than 30 pages exploring the importance of Nanih Waiya in the emergence and migration tales of the Choctaw. In the process, he presented stories that appeared to paint different images of the past.

One version of Choctaw origins focused on the mound itself and came from a Choctaw informant:

> A very long time ago the first creation of men was in Nanih
> Waiya; and there they were made and there they came forth.
> The Muscogees first came out of Nanih Waiya; and they then
> sunned themselves on Nanih Waiya's earthen rampart, and
> when they got dry they went to the east. On this side of the
> Tombigbee, there they rested and as they were smoking tobacco
> they dropped some fire. . . . The Cherokee next came out of
> Nanih Waiya. . . . And the Chickasaws third came out of Nanih
> Waiya. . . . And the Choctaws fourth and last came out of Nanih
> Waiya. And they then sunned themselves on the earthen ram-
> part and when they got dry, they did not go anywhere but set-
> tled down in this very land and it is the Choctaws' home.

Nanih Waiya also figured prominently in migration stories
that Swanton collected and published. The American artist George
Catlin recorded the following version in the 1830s:

> The Choctaws a great many winters ago commenced moving
> from the country where they then lived, which was a great dis-
> tance to the west of the great river and the mountains of snow,
> and they were a great many years on their way. A great medicine
> man led them the whole way, by going before with a red pole,
> which he stuck in the ground every night where they encamped.
> This pole was every morning found leaning to the east, and he
> told them that they must continue to travel to the east until
> the pole would stand upright in their encampment, and that
> there the Great Spirit had directed that they should live. At a
> place which they named *Nah-ne-wa-ye* (the sloping hill) the
> pole stood straight up, where they pitched their encampment,
> which was 1 mile square, with the men encamped on the out-
> side and the women and children in the center, which remains
> the center of the old Choctaw Nation.

Stories of emergence from the Mother Mound and a migration that ends at that same site may seem to present two contrast-
ing visions. However, both accounts emphasize Nanih Waiya as the
birthplace of the Choctaw in that land. Each story demonstrates

the rootedness of the Choctaw in Mississippi, where they resided before the removals of the nineteenth century. Therefore, in each narrative of Choctaw origins and in the years since the events described in those narratives, the Mother Mound provides a physical and symbolic anchor for Choctaw culture, identity, and worldview. It is where the Choctaw began their lives as a people.

MISSISSIPPIAN FOUNDATIONS

The emergence of the Choctaw as an established community can be traced through the use of archaeological and written records as well. Although pottery shards and journal accounts do not explain every stage of the historical process, it is clear that the Choctaw are connected to the Mississippian civilizations that dominated the landscape of the American southeast in the centuries before the arrival of the Europeans.

The mound-building civilizations that stretched from the Gulf of Mexico to the Great Lakes region rose in part because of the spread of maize, or corn. Archaeological evidence reveals the gradual development of corn cultivation in North America over a period of thousands of years. By A.D. 1000, corn became a critical agricultural foundation in the eastern half of the continent, and its cultivation had a substantial impact beyond its role as a food source. Greater reliance on agriculture allowed for a more sedentary lifestyle. A stable food source thus led to the development of larger and more organized societies. In the river valleys of the Southeast and elsewhere, populations grew, and people gathered in communities that were more politically and economically complex than those of previous centuries.

Cahokia was the largest of these civilizations. First established as a settlement in the mid-eighth century, Cahokia reached its height as a city during the peak of the Mississippian period, from about A.D. 1050 to 1275. It was located at the confluence of the Mississippi and Missouri Rivers, just east of present-day St. Louis. The city covered nearly 5 square miles (12.9 square kilometers, or sq. km), and scholars estimate that its population may have been as large as 40,000. Cahokia was also a planned urban landscape that contained more than 100 mounds. The largest of these mounds, called Monks Mound, loomed over a large, open plaza and had a base that measured 1,037 feet by 790 feet (316 by 240.8 m). Evidence from several Cahokia mounds has supported the existence of social and political hierarchies as well as substantial trade networks. Clearly the residents of that city lived in a structured society that had contact with other settlements located hundreds of miles away. Indeed, Cahokia's trade relations with other peoples provided access to copper, mica, seashells, and other goods not available in the immediate vicinity.

The Cahokia region is the site of an ancient city settled by the Mississippian peoples near Collinsville, Illinois. The base of Monks Mound is approximately the size of the Great Pyramid of Giza in Egypt.

The decline of this civilization began around 1275, and the city complex was abandoned by 1350 for reasons that remain uncertain. But the city's demise did not mean that other Mississippian settlements disappeared. Although they did not match the size of Cahokia, many of the smaller kingdoms that arose in the Southeast shared the elements of trade, architecture, and social organization illustrated at the confluence of the Missouri and Mississippi rivers. Scholars refer to the occurrence of these common symbolic elements as evidence of what they labeled the Southeastern Ceremonial Complex. At its core, this Southeastern Ceremonial Complex encompassed how the Mississippians distinguished rank and power in their societies. Images of falcons and engravings of the sun attested to political authority. Symbols of crosses and other illustrations of the four cardinal directions indicated common cosmological beliefs as well. Throughout the Mississippian chiefdoms, items engraved with these symbols were buried in the mounds of rulers and high priests to indicate their status.

These smaller kingdoms and independent towns were still in existence when Spanish conquistadores (explorers) first began their explorations into the interior of the North American mainland in the early sixteenth century. Ponce de León made the first recorded landing in Florida in 1513. But Hernando de Soto conducted the most intrusive campaign in the Southeast. He had already developed a reputation for brutality in earlier expeditions in what are now Nicaragua and Peru. From 1539 to 1542, de Soto and his force of 600 Spaniards made their way along a circuitous route that began on the lower Gulf Coast of present-day Florida, reached as far as present-day eastern Tennessee, and ended in the lower Mississippi Valley at the Gulf of Mexico. It was an arduous experience, and by the time their journey had ended, de Soto and nearly half of his men had died as a result of disease and violence.

The de Soto expedition had even more significant consequences for the indigenous inhabitants of the Southeast. The Spaniards sought gold and were willing to use any means to obtain it. Sometimes they presented gifts to town leaders they encountered, and sometimes they used brute force to conquer and pillage. De Soto's men captured and enslaved as many as 2,000 American Indians from the Alabama-Mississippi region alone. In addition, an estimated 3,000 to 5,000 American Indians in that same region lost their lives to Spanish aggression. Similar to other European excursions in the Americas, de Soto's men also brought widespread death through disease. A lack of immunity to smallpox and measles, among other European diseases, wreaked havoc among the indigenous populations of the Southeast in the wake of de Soto's campaign.

At the time de Soto's expedition moved through the Alabama-Mississippi region, only smaller chiefdoms and towns dotted the landscape. Indeed, for most of the Mississippian period leading up to this time, the bulk of what would become the Choctaw homeland was uninhabited. As a result, though the Spaniards encountered a number of different peoples, they had no interactions with an indigenous community known as Choctaw. European intrusions into the interior of the Southeast were nearly nonexistent for the next 100 years. Until the late seventeenth century, therefore, the inhabitants of this region had little contact with European outsiders. Yet when a party of Frenchmen led by Pierre Le Moyne d'Iberville arrived in 1699, they came across a group of people who referred to themselves as Choctaw.

The years between the journeys of de Soto and d'Iberville had witnessed a substantial shift in the region's social and political organization. Most importantly, it was during that period that the Choctaw became a people. Although scholars have been unable to pinpoint specific territorial boundaries for the community, the Choctaw were known to be a confederacy of people who lived south of the Chickasaw, east of the Natchez, and west of the Alabama. This gave the Choctaw confederacy a territory that covered most of present-day Mississippi from Hattiesburg in the south to the southern banks of the Big Black River that crosses the central

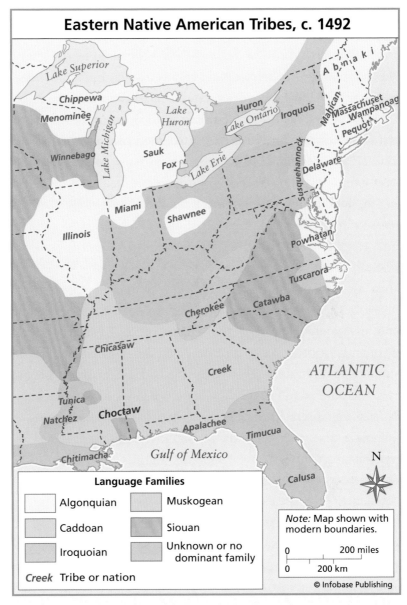

Eastern Native American Tribes, c. 1492

Lake Superior

Chippewa
Menominee

Winnebago

Lake Michigan

Sauk
Fox

Lake Huron

Lake Erie

Huron

Lake Ontario

Iroquois

A b n a k i

Mahican

Massachuset
Wampanoag
Pequot

Susquehannock

Delaware

Miami

Illinois

Shawnee

Powhatan

Tuscarora

Cherokee

Catawba

Chicasaw

Creek

ATLANTIC
OCEAN

Tunica

Natchez

Choctaw

Apalachee

Timucua

Chitimacha

Gulf of Mexico

Calusa

N

Language Families

- Algonquian
- Caddoan
- Iroquoian
- Muskogean
- Siouan
- Unknown or no dominant family

Creek Tribe or nation

Note: Map shown with modern boundaries.

0 ———— 200 miles
0 ———— 200 km

© Infobase Publishing

The Choctaw people are members of the Muskogean language family. They descended from a mound-building culture called the Mississippians, who settled in the southeastern United States. The Choctaw traded with neighboring tribes in the southeast, especially the Chickasaw. Long ago, the Choctaw and the Chickasaw were part of the same tribe.

portion of the state. According to many accounts, this fledgling Choctaw confederacy had even established a measure of control over the Tombigbee River region that reaches into northeastern Mississippi near Tupelo. Written and archaeological records indicate that the Choctaw had migrated into this area in the aftermath of the first Spanish expeditions in the sixteenth century. At first glance, then, the Choctaw confederacy encompassed towns consisting of remnants from earlier Mississippian societies and chiefdoms.

These remnant groups served as the foundation for what became the three recognized divisions of the Choctaw confederacy. Peoples who had lived along the upper Pearl River near Jackson, Mississippi, and the western tributaries of the Tombigbee River moved eastward, and their villages made up the Western Division. The Choctaw referred to them as Okla Falaya, or "people who are widely dispersed." The villages of the Eastern Division encompassed the Burial Urn people, who were descendants of the Moundville civilization. They were called Okla Tannap, or "people from the other side." Finally, the Sixtowns Division was made up of those who migrated from the lower Pearl River in the vicinity of Columbia, Mississippi, and the Mobile River in present-day western Alabama. The Choctaw designation for this division was Okla Hannali, or "people of six towns."

CREATION OF THE CHOCTAW CONFEDERACY

Evidence of this Choctaw emergence is based on cultural elements as well. These elements both connect the Choctaw and link their origin to the Southeastern Ceremonial Complex identified in the previous centuries. These developments are particularly important. As historian and anthropologist Patricia Galloway notes in *Choctaw Genesis*, "The Choctaws did not exist as an ethnic group . . . until they *decided* that they existed as a group." This final piece of Choctaw emergence, therefore, examines the manner in which these migratory Mississippian groups surrendered many of their distinctive rituals and cultural traits and adopted a set of uniform ceremonies and practices.

The three principal geographic districts of the Choctaw confederacy provided geographic, political, and social structures for the confederacy. The workings of the confederacy did not take shape overnight, and they built on preexisting foundations. One noted continuity with a Mississippian past was a distinctive social and political division. Historian Greg O'Brien has asserted that the Choctaw confederacy encompassed a prominent ethnic divide that continued well into the eighteenth century. The Imoklasha and Inhulahta divisions were important ethnic structures. Entire villages in each of the three divisions were one or the other. Recorded interactions with Europeans indicate that the Imoklasha controlled the Western Division and the Inhulahta controlled the Eastern Division. The two ethnic divisions also encompassed a number of *iksas*, or clans. Though the exact roles of these clans remain unclear, they contributed another level of kinship ties within Choctaw towns and divisions.

The Inhulahta were considered to be the elder brothers of the Imoklasha, a relationship that granted them prominence and seniority. But both divisions supplied leaders to the confederacy as a whole. Both the Inhulahta and the Imoklasha provided civil chiefs, war leaders, and shamans. No single division dominated in peace or war, and each division had a chief. That meant that negotiations with outside forces usually included representatives from the Western, Eastern, and Sixtown divisions. No single individual could lay claim to leadership of the Choctaw confederacy. The position of chief in each division appeared to be a hereditary office. The same was true of the subordinate peace and war chiefs.

The women of the different divisions played a crucial role in the early efforts to unite these disparate groups. The construction of the Choctaw confederacy required negotiation and did not occur without substantial effort. In many cases, the negotiations included intermarriage among the different migratory communities. In particular, unions between male leaders of one community and the daughters or sisters of prominent men in another community created important social and political bonds. Yet women shaped the early confederacy through more than just marriage. Matrilineal kinship was an integral element that bound the Choctaw together. This meant that kinship ties through mothers and maternal uncles established lines of descent and influenced the distribution of land. This kinship structure therefore granted women influence over key aspects of Choctaw society.

Female influence was evident in the material culture of the people who became Choctaw. One example is the pottery style that developed over time. Archaeologists have shown that a unique Choctaw design gradually grew out of what were once the distinct styles of the respective migratory groups. Women also played a critical role in supplying the basic needs of the community. The Choctaw lived off what they could obtain through hunting, fishing, and farming, and women were in charge of the fields. Corn was the most important crop, but the Choctaw also grew beans, melons, pumpkins, peas, and sunflowers. And while hunting was important, the produce of these small gardens provided more than half of the food for daily life. Traditional dishes like tafula, a dish of boiled pounded corn, were mainstays of the Choctaw diet. In addition, Choctaw women used the products of the hunt to feed and clothe themselves and their families. In the late seventeenth and early eighteenth centuries, this meant that the hides, bones, teeth, and claws of both bear and deer were the most common source of clothing, shoes, and ornamentation.

The Choctaw lived in homes that reflected their surroundings, as well. Wood and bark from pine and cypress trees were common materials used to build the small cabins in which they lived. Mud and wooden posts buried into the ground formed the base of the house that usually had a thatched roof. Seats and beds made of cane were the primary pieces of furniture inside an early eighteenth-century Choctaw dwelling. According to Swanton, one

The Choctaw lived in villages of houses made of plaster and rivercane walls, with thatched roofs. If the village was located on the border, reinforced walls were built around the village for protection. Most Choctaw towns also had a ball field for stickball games.

Choctaw informant stated that the north wall of each house was the strongest, built that way to protect the inhabitants from what was considered the unhealthy north wind.

This material culture was important to daily life, but oral communication was another significant factor in the creation of the Choctaw confederacy. When Europeans arrived in the Southeast, most of the indigenous inhabitants belonged to the Muskogean language family. As a result, the Mississippian groups that came together in the Choctaw confederacy already spoke languages that were related to one another. Because they could understand one another, there was not any substantial alteration of their respective dialects during the initial union. However, the Choctaw adopted a common language for external relationships and diplomacy. Consequently, what outsiders called the Choctaw language was the one selected as most useful for formal interactions.

A unified worldview and the rituals necessary to ground this worldview were another essential component of the confederacy. One of the most notable rituals involved the Choctaw system of burial. The Choctaw chose to adopt a single form of burial that had been reserved for elites in the mound-building societies of the Southeastern Ceremonial Complex. The practice is known as secondary burial processing. The dead individual was first placed upon a tall scaffold, and while his or her physical body rotted, the spirit wandered. The secondary burial processing occurred when the remains of the body were taken from the scaffold. As the spirit made its way to the next world, the bones were stripped clean, and the skeleton was laid to rest in a charnel house or burial mound. Although the remains of elites received more time and effort in this particular practice, all Choctaw were beneficiaries. This ritual clearly illustrated the Choctaw belief in a spiritual world and the need to conduct the dead properly to the afterlife.

Like many other Southeastern Indian peoples, the Choctaw also conducted an annual Green Corn Ceremony. This celebration of the first corn harvest of the season provided an opportunity to cleanse and renew. Men and women gathered worn-out clothes and other items to rid their homes and their towns of filth. It was both a physical and religious effort to get rid of any pollution that tainted their relationship with one another and with their sacred world. With its emphasis on corn, this ceremony also particularly honored the work and place of Choctaw women. Their efforts and their role in the community were at the heart of the Green Corn Ceremony.

Burial rituals and annual ceremonies were simply one more way in which the Choctaw bound their society together at a village and division level. More importantly, they reflected the choices made and the actions taken by the Choctaw to create their confederacy. It was a gradual process that began in the aftermath of de Soto's expedition and remained a work in progress when the French arrived more than a century and a half later.

The history of the Choctaw emergence rests on a diverse foundation of oral, archaeological, and written sources. Through geography and politics as well as social and cultural practices, disparate remnant groups of declining Mississippian civilizations formed the Choctaw confederacy over the course of the seventeenth century. The development of this alliance occurred at a time of increased European interference in the interior lands of the Southeast. Its structures were neither fully formed nor completely cohesive at the time that the French and English entered the scene in the early 1700s. However, the confederacy was developed enough to be a recognizable institution to outsiders. From their homes in the vicinity of Nanih Waiya, the Choctaw stood ready to confront and manage the return of the European outsiders.

The Choctaw
in Colonial
North America

The world into which the Choctaw emerged changed in fundamental ways in the eighteenth century. The arrival of Pierre Le Moyne d'Iberville's expedition of Frenchmen in 1699 did more than just signal the entrance of the French into a region already touched by the English and the Spanish. Indeed, the French advance marked the beginning of nearly seven decades of trade, diplomacy, and violence that would shake the foundations of the newly emergent Choctaw people. In the early 1700s, the Choctaw built trade relationships, and in the 1760s, they struggled to manage the impact of the Seven Years' War. Through these and many other experiences, they fought to maintain and protect the boundaries of their land, politics, and culture.

CHOCTAW AND EUROPEANS

The French entrance into the lower Mississippi Valley boded well for the Choctaw initially. When d'Iberville established what became known as Fort Biloxi, the site of present-day Biloxi, Mississippi, he thrust the French into a region already feeling the effects of European colonization. For nearly a decade, the Choctaw had been fighting their Chickasaw neighbors, who raided the Choctaw villages for captives. The Chickasaw raiders proceeded to sell those captives to English traders, who then shipped them off as slaves to Caribbean plantations. D'Iberville and his compatriots represented an opportunity to alter this balance of power. The Choctaw hoped that an alliance with the French would ultimately help them to resist the Chickasaw and their English allies.

The Choctaw-French alliance was framed by each side's perceptions and expectations. From the Choctaw perspective, their relationship with the French was based on their ability to provide what the Choctaw needed. In 1699, the Choctaw needed guns, gunpowder, and bullets to combat the Chickasaw warriors, who were supplied by the English. But the French also had expectations and demands of their own. As part of a material exchange for the goods they provided, the French desired items they could sell in Europe. In the early 1700s, deerskins were the most marketable product from this American Indian trade. Just as important, the French expected the Choctaw to support French interests in the region. This specifically meant that the French counted on their Choctaw trading partners to fight on their side in any future conflicts against the Spanish or English.

Yet the structure of this relationship between the French and the Choctaw was not as simple as either party anticipated or wanted. Through the world of trade, the Choctaw became involved in European power struggles to a greater extent than they could have imagined. It would prove disastrous to the Choctaw. For the French, the relationship created numerous problems as well. In particular, despite their wishes to the contrary, they were never able to deal with a central Choctaw government. The three divisions within the Choctaw confederacy made their own decisions and pursued their respective agendas as they deemed necessary. In many instances, the motivations and goals of the three divisions did not match.

The presence of the English and the Spanish in the region made it easier for the three Choctaw divisions to maintain a measure of independence. Choctaw leaders had options available to

After Hernando de Soto's campaign through the Alabama-Mississippi region, Europeans avoided the interior of the Southeast. Therefore, contact was limited between the Europeans and indigenous peoples. Pierre Le Moyne d'Iberville's expedition of Frenchmen in 1699 dramatically altered the Choctaw way of life.

them and did not have to trade with the French or do only what the French wanted them to do. Therefore, Choctaw complaints about the prices of French goods often represented vague or specific threats to open trade relations with the English colonists in the Carolinas or the English traders living in the Chickasaw and Creek villages. During the late 1730s and into the 1740s, several prominent men from the Western Choctaw towns even attempted to secure the English trade through treaty agreements when the French refused to cooperate.

The French presence affected more than just Choctaw politics. As historian Michelene E. Pesantubbee argues in *Choctaw Women in a Chaotic World*, ongoing relations with French officials and Jesuit priests gradually altered the place and role of women in Choctaw society. The French came from a male-dominated society and tried to impose their beliefs on their political allies and trading partners. Indeed, Pesantubbee concludes that "women's economic, political, and domestic life had changed so much during the first half of the eighteenth century that ceremonies such as the Green Corn Ceremony did not survive." As Choctaw society adapted to external pressures like French expectations, fundamental parts of their world changed.

INTER-INDIAN RELATIONS

Diplomacy, trade, and warfare were not actions limited to the Choctaw and Europeans. But inter-Indian relations in the lower Mississippi Valley of the eighteenth century were difficult to separate from the European colonial presence. Interactions with American Indian tribes like the Chickasaw and the Creek were also a crucial part of Choctaw diplomacy. However, the respective connections to the British and the French played substantial roles in the manner in which the Choctaw got along with their American Indian neighbors.

Because of proximity and their respective ties to the European colonists, the Chickasaw Indians figured most prominently in Choctaw diplomatic affairs in the early 1700s. The Chickasaw and Choctaw shared some common traits. Their languages were similar enough that they could understand each other, and both societies were matrilineal. In addition, the Chickasaw had a decentralized political structure. Like the Choctaw, therefore, individual leaders headed each of the Chickasaw villages, and there was no single Chickasaw chief. Because the Chickasaw emphasized military prowess among their young men, they often fought with their neighbors. And when they learned that their new English allies would purchase American Indian captives, Chickasaw warriors were happy to profit from this slave trade. Only the arrival of the French and their trade goods allowed the Choctaw to fight back effectively against the powerful Chickasaw.

During the first half of the eighteenth century, the Choctaw and Chickasaw fought each other even as they struggled to negotiate away from European influences. In 1720, for example, conflict arose when Chickasaw warriors killed a Frenchman they accused of being a spy. The French then sent weapons and ammunition to the Choctaw towns and urged their allies to avenge this murder. For the next several years, the Chickasaw and Choctaw fought each other because of the French desire for revenge. Hostilities only ended when the Choctaw and Chickasaw arranged a peace council in 1724. Although the French wanted the war to continue, the Choctaw and Chickasaw desired a truce. The negotiations between the tribes forced the French to accept this peace the following year.

What the 1724 episode indicates is that despite the intrusive presence of the French and English, there were elements of inter-Indian diplomacy that functioned outside of this European presence. One prominent example of American Indian structured diplomacy was the position titled *fanimingo*, which literally means "squirrel chief." A fanimingo was an individual within a town who had been adopted by a neighboring tribe. His role was to advocate in favor of his adopted tribe when the possibility of war arose. For example, a Choctaw town would have a fanimingo within a neighboring Chickasaw town, and the Chickasaw would have one within a Choctaw town. Although a fanimingo might not be able to prevent war, the councils of each community would have to hear his perspective before they made their decision. It was an important institution that existed outside the realm of European trade goods and manipulation.

In addition to the fanimingo, the decentralized nature of Choctaw and Chickasaw politics allowed for the possibility of alliance between individual villages. One of the most notable examples of this came when a Choctaw warrior named Red Shoe attempted to build an alliance with the Chickasaw and the English traders living nearby. Red Shoe was a warrior who had gained prominence in battles against the Chickasaw in the early 1730s. Because of his success, he demanded better terms in his dealings with the French. When they failed to meet his demands, Red Shoe chose to turn to the Chickasaw and their English allies. He had the support of many men and women from his home in the western towns, for they believed his actions would benefit them all.

This move by Red Shoe and his supporters illustrated that the Choctaw could not operate completely free from the meddling of the Europeans. Even as he attempted to take advantage of Choctaw and Chickasaw politics, French and English traders and diplomats sought to control the affairs of their American Indian allies. In the end, European demands for Choctaw allegiance and Red Shoe's desire to forge a different path helped lead to civil war among the Choctaw towns.

CHOCTAW CIVIL WAR

Two main issues rested at the core of what is known as the Choctaw Civil War. First and foremost, by the 1740s, American Indian and European diplomacy were intricately connected because of decades of trade, politics, and warfare. Second, despite the decades of interaction, Europeans and American Indians continued to misunderstand each other's motives and actions.

The specific spark for war arose from the measures taken by Red Shoe. His attempts to build an alliance with the English had angered not only the Choctaw leaders of the eastern towns but also their French allies. It was not surprising, therefore, that in the summer of 1746, Choctaw warriors from the eastern towns killed a Chickasaw diplomat and his wife who had traveled to Red Shoe to affirm their relationship. In response, Red Shoe killed three Frenchmen and sent their scalps to the English and Chickasaw to demonstrate his devotion to their alliance.

Red Shoe's retaliation addressed two important issues. First, he avenged the murder of the Chickasaw man and woman with the death of a common enemy. Second, he accomplished that revenge without killing other Choctaw. The French did not see these actions in the same light. Instead, they demanded that Alibamon Mingo and other eastern Choctaw leaders attack the western towns to kill Red Shoe and all other Choctaw headmen responsible for the deaths of the three Frenchmen. Alibamon Mingo was reluctant to act on these French demands because such attacks were outside of the cultural practices of the Choctaw. The Choctaw did not allow for the deaths of other Choctaw in exchange for the deaths of outsiders.

Yet both French and English demands ultimately led to war. The French refused to provide trade goods to the eastern towns until Alibamon Mingo and the Eastern Choctaw attacked. Red Shoe in particular needed to die before the French would be satisfied. At the same time, the Western Choctaw moved quickly to affirm their allegiance to the English in order to gain access to more trade goods. For both the English and the French, this war was less about the Choctaw and more about their respective colonial interests. The French wanted to make sure that the English did not have the upper hand in the region, and the English wanted to make sure that the French did not. Both European powers were willing to use the Choctaw to accomplish that goal. And although the Choctaw were reluctant to act on these external demands, their desire for alliance and the trade goods it provided overcame their concerns.

The war between the Eastern and Western Choctaw factions lasted until the late fall of 1750. Red Shoe was killed in the summer of 1747, but hostilities continued for another three years. War parties on both sides destroyed entire villages and burned fields of ripened corn. By 1749, it was clear that the Eastern Choctaw were winning as the Western Choctaw struggled to obtain the necessary supplies from their English allies. When Alibamon Mingo presented the skulls of three prominent western chiefs to the French governor, Pierre de Rigaud, Marquis de Vaudreuil, at the end of 1749, it was clear the war would not last much longer.

Yet the peace that came at the end of this civil war did not end the tension within the Choctaw villages. Defeat did not eliminate English influence, and the divide between the Eastern and Western Choctaw factions continued to exist. As a result, the onset of war between the French and the English in 1754 brought change once again to the lower Mississippi Valley.

FROM THE SEVEN YEARS' WAR TO THE AMERICAN REVOLUTION

The main theaters of the Seven Years' War in North America were located hundreds of miles away from the Choctaw homelands. Violence flared in the Great Lakes region, and conflict in the Southeast occurred almost exclusively in Cherokee territory in the Carolinas and present-day eastern Tennessee. Yet, although the war did not range into the lower Mississippi Valley, the impacts of the conflict reached far beyond the sites of actual violence. With the Treaty of Paris in 1763, the British assumed authority over great expanses of what was once New France. They now claimed the eastern half of the continent right up to the Mississippi River. And the Choctaw, who had grown accustomed to choosing between the British and the French, now had limited options.

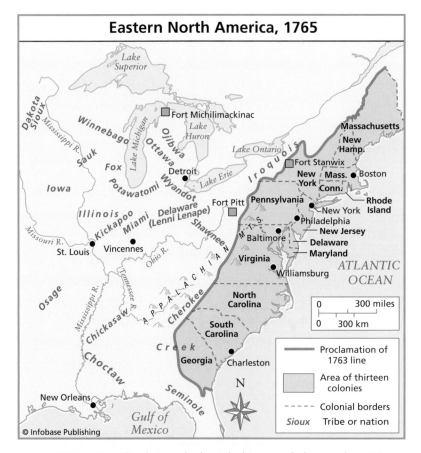

From 1700 to 1763, the Choctaw had good relations with the French. In 1763, due to the Treaty of Paris, the French lost control over large areas of North America. The British now claimed the eastern half of the United States. In March 1765, the Choctaw and the British worked out a treaty that defined the eastern and southern boundaries of the Choctaw Nation.

Under the peace treaty that ended the war, Choctaw territory was now part of what the British called West Florida. British officials soon learned that most Choctaw expected them to fulfill the responsibilities once carried by the French in the region. In 1765, Choctaw representatives met in council with British officials at Mobile. Chickasaw and Creek leaders were also present, and the Indians formalized their relations with the British authorities. A chief from the Sixtowns named Tomatly Mingo made Choctaw expectations clear. "If I am become their Son," Tomatly Mingo asserted, "they must Act the Part of a Father in Supplying my Wants by proper Presents and also by furnishing a plentyfull Trade." In other words, the British should not expect the Choctaw to submit to their demands simply because the French had left the region.

Choctaw desires and needs made it necessary to demand generosity from the British. Most importantly, Choctaw leaders required access to material goods to consolidate their positions of authority. French gift-giving habits had enabled Choctaw leaders to distribute wealth within their communities and thus retain their political influence. But British officials in West Florida declared that they were not the French and they would not be so liberal about giving gifts to their Indian allies. Similar British policies north of the Ohio River had led to the uprising known as Pontiac's War in 1763. Within the West Florida region, however, the policy had a different impact.

Choctaw leaders were most concerned about their ability to control their young men. Without material goods to support their efforts, leaders would have little influence, and the young warriors might cause trouble. In particular, young warriors in search of honor might provoke war with the British through attacks on traders or British colonists. The solution to this problem came in the form of intertribal warfare. Choctaw leaders of all three divisions realized that they could maintain their authority and protect their trade relations with the British by channeling the desires and needs of the young warriors by warring against the Creek Indians.

From 1765 to 1776, Choctaw and Creek warriors waged war in the Southeast. The conflict revealed almost unprecedented unity among the Choctaw divisions. Warriors from the western towns, eastern towns, and Sixtowns participated in attacks against Creek war parties and villages. Choctaw leaders also used the heightened state of warfare to increase demands on British officials for guns,

Tomatly Mingo Speaks in April 1765

In the spring of 1765, English officials held a council with the Choctaw and Chickasaw in an attempt to bring peace to the Southeast. It had been two years since the British and French had signed the Treaty of Paris in 1763. British officials were still attempting to impose their authority over Indians like the Choctaw and Chickasaw. Agent John Stuart intended to use this council to inform the Indians about how the British would handle business with the departure of the French.

Tomatly Mingo was a chief from the Sixtowns and was the most senior member of the Imoklasha. Therefore, he had the privilege of speaking first for the Choctaw. His response illustrated that the Choctaw were not going to submit to British authority. They had a great deal of experience with Europeans and wanted to make their position clear. The following is an excerpt from Tomatly Mingo's statement to the British on April 1, 1765.

> I am the first of the race of Imongolatcha, it is true I am a poor Red Man who came into the World Naked, and since my rising into Manhood have Acquired no Necessary Arts

ammunition, and other trade goods. They effectively used the displays of martial prowess by their young men to show the British why they should not forsake their Choctaw trading partners.

British contributions to the Choctaw military efforts were not a blind response to the demands of Choctaw leaders, however. The Choctaw-Creek War also served British interests. The Seven Years' War had created a substantial debt, and throughout the 1760s, the British struggled to put their finances in order. Consequently, they did not have the necessary financial or military resources to

to Supply those Wants; Yet I am going to deliver my Senti-
ments to my Father Boldly as a man who does not regard
trifling Inconvenience.

It is the Custom of the Red Men to take Preceedence
according to their Seniority, I am of the Race of Imongo-
latcha & in Consequence the Second Rank in the Chactaw
Nation, The Race of Ingholakta is before me, but on this
day being Investd by the Consent of the Chiefs with the
Authority of the Pipe and other ensigns of Peace, I now
take place of Alibamo Mingo, Altho I acknowledge him to
be my Superior. . . .

I now Speak for all the Chiefs and Warriors of my
Nation, we thank the Great King for sending a father
amongst us, you have undoubtedly Run great Risques in
coming here, & it is to be Supposed as you come to Supply
all our Wants, you have brought Guns Cloathing and other
Necessaries. . . .

I was formerly a Frenchman now they have abandoned
me and left me to the English, how many times is it Necessary I should declare myself an Englishman. You Favre was
formerly French, now you are become English, and if I am
become their Son, they must Act the Part of a Father in Supplying my Wants by proper Presents and also by furnishing a plentyfull Trade.

impose their will on any of the Indian communities in the Southeast. They could, however, supply and support both the Creek and
Choctaw. This would ensure a continuation of the war and would
make a strong British military presence unnecessary. British officials even removed soldiers from West Florida during the first
years of the war.

The conflict between the Choctaw and the Creek Indians
signified several important trends following the departure of the
French. First, the desire for European material goods continued

to influence Choctaw actions. Without the option of turning to the French, it became better to wage war against Indian neighbors than to undermine trade relations with the British. Second, it had become nearly impossible to separate inter-Indian diplomacy from relations with the British or other European nations.

THE END OF THE CHOCTAW-CREEK WAR

It is not a coincidence that the Choctaw-Creek War finally came to an end when it did. In October 1776, when Choctaw and Creek delegates met in Pensacola, Florida, to engage in peace negotiations, the British were once again involved. The British Indian agent for the Choctaw and Chickasaw, John Stuart, had his orders to promote peace among the Southeastern Indians so that they would be available to support British efforts against the colonists, who had declared their independence. The British were now prepared to provide gifts to ensure that the Choctaw would fight a different war for them.

Stuart's diplomatic efforts were only the latest in a series of negotiations between the Choctaw and various European powers in the eighteenth century. From 1699 to 1776, the different parties struggled to control the terms of their respective relationships. At the outbreak of the American Revolution, it was not clear how much influence and independence the Choctaw would maintain in the midst of one more power struggle.

The Choctaw
and the
American Republic

The American Revolution has always been described, and rightly so, as a momentous occasion and a critical turning point in the history of the United States. It served as the birth of the American nation and the forge for the principles on which the country is governed. The American Revolution is important to the Choctaw as well, but for very different reasons. On the one hand, the creation of the United States started one more chapter in the Choctaw's longer history of economic, cultural, and political encounters with outsiders. On the other hand, the end of the war and the subsequent departure of the British marked a significant change for the Choctaw and their neighbors in the Southeast. The United States and its citizens could not be ignored. In the early decades of the American republic, the Choctaw did what they could to adapt to the new balance of power in the lower Mississippi Valley.

AFTER THE AMERICAN REVOLUTION

At the onset of the American Revolution, the Thirteen Colonies did not have sufficient resources to forge an alliance with the American Indians living on their borders. Nor did the colonists in the Carolinas and Georgia have a strong interest in befriending any of the southeastern tribes. As a result, Choctaw warriors fought alongside their British allies in the early years of the Revolutionary War. A party of 155 Choctaw men under the leadership of the Western Division headman Franchimastabé traveled to Natchez in 1778. They went to this town located on the Mississippi River about 100 miles (161 km) north of present-day Baton Rouge, Louisiana, in an effort to capture a raiding party of American colonists. These Choctaw then remained in Natchez for more than a month to safeguard the region from further American attacks. The Choctaw alliance with the British also brought them into conflict with the Spanish, who had sided with the Americans. Yet the autonomy of the three Choctaw divisions remained intact. Warriors from the Sixtowns actually joined with the Spanish in battles against the British along the Gulf Coast.

For the most part, however, the violence of the American Revolution did not intrude into Choctaw territory. More important to Choctaw autonomy and the integrity of their territory were the consequences of the revolution. When British and American diplomats signed the treaty that ended the war for independence, the Choctaw world changed once again. No longer were the British going to be an influential presence in the region. Only the Spanish and the Americans remained.

In the 1783 Treaty of Paris, the British surrendered most of the territory east of the Mississippi River to the United States. Despite this dramatic departure of the British, the decade after the end of the American Revolution also witnessed a measure of continuity. Most importantly, the three Choctaw divisions sought to build alliances through customary means. Choctaw men and women still desired the goods obtained through trade, and they needed to find new partners to fulfill those needs. Proximity led the Western

During the American Revolution, most of the southeastern tribes sided with the British against the Thirteen Colonies, while others remained neutral. Some Choctaw warriors were hired to patrol the Mississippi River against American attacks. Above, British general John Burgoyne secures an alliance with Southeastern Indians.

Choctaw towns to turn initially to the Spanish, who still had claim to the territory west of the Mississippi River.

A series of agreements negotiated by the Choctaw in the last two decades of the eighteenth century provide greater insight into their diplomatic efforts. By all accounts, the Choctaw intended to maintain a strong position between the Americans and the Spanish. Consequently, no single treaty gave the indication that the Choctaw wanted to befriend only the Americans or the Spanish. The first agreement the Choctaw signed with the United States came in 1786 with the Treaty of Hopewell. At this conference, Benjamin Hawkins and two other government-appointed treaty commissioners sought to establish a strong trade relationship with the Choctaw. All three Choctaw divisions were represented at this council. However, these negotiations occurred little more than a year after Franchimastabé and the Western Choctaw had held a council with Spanish officials in Mobile, Alabama. Therefore, although the Choctaw delegation at Hopewell pledged perpetual peace and friendship with the United States in 1786, they balanced these pledges with an ongoing relationship with the Spanish. As of the late 1780s, they did not see a need to choose one over the other.

The first sign that the Choctaw might not be able to maintain this diplomatic balance came with the Treaty of San Lorenzo in 1795. This pact was negotiated between Spain and the United States. Its primary purpose was to set the boundaries between

Puckshunubbee Speaks at Fort Adams

In 1801, three American commissioners met in council with Choctaw leaders. They met at Fort Adams, an American outpost just down the Mississippi River from Natchez. That council led to what is known as the Fort Adams treaty of 1801. The American treaty commissioners were seeking land cessions and permission to build a road through Choctaw territory.

The following is an excerpt of comments made by a Choctaw chief from the Western Division named Puckshunubbee on December 13, 1801, four days before the Choctaw signed the treaty. Puckshunubbee was one of 13 Choctaw who spoke at the council. In the decades that followed this treaty, he would be one of the Choctaw chiefs who adopted cotton cultivation and supported missionary schools even as he sought to limit the intrusions of the American government and its citizens.

The old line that the other chiefs repeated, as far as I understood from my forefathers, I will name its course and the water-courses it crosses, beginning at the Homochitto, the Spanish and American territories in the Southeast. Although the treaty did not remove the Spanish from the region, it laid the foundation for an increased American presence in the Southeast. Indeed, the creation of Mississippi Territory in April 1798 indicated that the United States had plans for the region. Then, in 1801, the Choctaw signed a treaty that ceded more than 2.5 million acres (1 million ha) and granted permission to the Americans to build a road through their lands to Mississippi Territory. Additional treaties negotiated in 1803 and 1805 also included sizable land cessions to the United States. It was clear that the Choctaw were going to have their hands full with their new neighbors.

running thence nearly a northwest course, until it strikes the Standing-pines creek; thence, crosses the Bayou Pierre, high up, and Big Black; from thence, strikes the Mississippi at the mouth of Tallauhatche (Yawzoo). That line I wish may be renewed that both parties may know their own. There are people over, or on the line; it is my wish they may be removed immediately. Where the line runs, along the Bayour Pierre, some whites are settled on this line, and some over it; those over, I wish may be removed. If there are none over, there is nothing spoiled. From the information I have received from my forefathers, this Natchez country belonged to red people; the whole of it, which is now settled by white people. But you Americans were not the first people who got this country from the red people. We sold our lands, but never got any value for it; this I speak from the information of old men. We did not sell them to you, and, as we never received any thing for it, I wish you, our friends, to think of it, and make us some compensation for it. We are red people, and you are white people; we did not come here to beg; we brought no property with us to purchase any thing; we came to do the business of our nation and return.

POWER IN CHOCTAW SOCIETY

The Choctaw had begun to adjust to their changing world even before the negotiation of the Treaty of San Lorenzo and the changes it brought to the Southeast. One of the critical elements of change occurred in the area of political power and leadership. Although the three divisions still existed, in the late eighteenth century, Choctaw political power became more centralized. The second critical element of change developed within the familiar setting of trade relations. Leadership continued to depend on access to the material goods produced through strong trade relations. However, the increased presence of American traders made it difficult for leaders to control the distribution of those valuable trade goods.

The autonomy of the three divisions of Choctaw villages defined Choctaw politics for much of the eighteenth century. No single chief, division, or other political entity controlled the decisions or actions of all the Choctaw, but that began to change in the decades after the American Revolution. More and more, the interactions between Choctaw chiefs and outsiders indicated that the divisions were beginning to unite into a more centralized confederacy. By the 1810s, though it was still an exaggeration to say the Choctaw had become a nation, the autonomous divisions were gradually becoming a political element of decreasing influence.

This development in the Choctaw political structure was in part a response to the diplomatic and economic shift brought about by the Treaty of San Lorenzo. The curtailed Spanish presence meant that all Choctaw chiefs turned to the Americans for the political and economic influence they desired. The treaty councils held with American officials in the first decade of the nineteenth century included representatives from all the Choctaw divisions. And as historian James Taylor Carson states, while such events did not create a Choctaw nation overnight, "they did crystallize a sense of common purpose among the chiefs." Instead of three divisions competing for alliances, the Western, Eastern, and

Sixtowns Choctaw now began to recognize their mutual interests in the face of an expanding American nation. They realized that they could more effectively represent Choctaw interests if they acted together.

This gradual move toward a centralization of political power was important in part because two factors had changed in relation to trade and the Choctaw. First, young men had increased access to traders and therefore did not have to rely on the chiefs to provide and distribute material goods. Second, those trade goods and the pursuit of them had become a familiar and at times negative influence in Choctaw daily life.

Traders and their merchandise had become more accessible before the American Revolution. With the departure of the French after the Seven Years' War, in fact, Choctaw leaders lost a measure of their influence. British traders living in Choctaw villages still worked closely with the local chiefs. But other merchants without local ties had no such restrictions. By the 1770s, many young Choctaw men dealt directly with these outsiders and bypassed the usual management of their leaders. This independence weakened the traditional forms of political influence within Choctaw villages.

As a result, some prominent Choctaw chiefs in the late eighteenth century tied their political and economic fortunes even closer to traders than ever before. Franchimastabé made a point of ritually adopting those merchants who chose to reside in his village. By developing such close relationships, he hoped to develop strong ties that even the changing circumstances could not weaken. Such adoptions were not a radical new approach by Choctaw chiefs. Ritual adoption was often used to create a relationship in which Euro-American traders were expected to grant protectors like Franchimastabé special rights. However, the emphasis on such associations reflected the concerns of the men who formerly controlled access to trade goods without exception.

The Choctaw gained considerable wealth and political power through trading relationships with different European groups. After the American Revolution, the Americans displaced English and Spanish traders and made trade goods available to the Choctaw at lower prices.

Just as problematic for Choctaw society were the changes wrought by the pursuit of these goods. Young men with direct access to traders now had an increased motivation to participate in this method of exchange. Because both British and American traders desired deerskins, the result was an increase in hunting. Young Choctaw men began to overhunt their customary territories and soon had to travel farther and farther to obtain the skins necessary to purchase the goods they desired. This could lead to conflict with neighboring tribes and also lengthened the duration of the hunt, which in turn affected the seasonal subsistence patterns of all Choctaw.

Increased access to goods also meant that more European- and American-made goods were present in Choctaw society. Items that were once considered rare or even supernatural had become more ordinary. Just as those who once controlled access to these goods began to lose authority, so did the goods themselves lose a measure of their power. At the same time, the increased presence of alcohol produced an entirely different result. By the late eighteenth century, alcohol had become a divisive and disruptive force in Choctaw society. In particular, the consumption of alcohol had a tendency to increase the number of violent encounters between young Choctaw men and others in and out of the Choctaw villages.

THE CHOCTAW ECONOMY

The presence of more than just alcohol had initiated a gradual transformation of Choctaw society by the early nineteenth century. Although the foundation of the Choctaw village economy did not change, key elements did. In particular, new agricultural methods and crops altered the look of Choctaw settlements and approaches to subsistence. Just as important, the growth of a Choctaw marketplace society had an impact on the roles and responsibilities of men and women throughout the region. Men and women still lived according to Choctaw cultural norms, but they found new ways to participate in the developing regional economy.

Historian James Carson describes the early-nineteenth-century economy of the Choctaw as one that rested in between the nonmarket economy of their past and the market economy that characterized American society. Most important to this distinction were the aspects of Choctaw life that did not change. Even as the Choctaw became more active in pursuing trade opportunities, they maintained facets of their customary gendered division of labor. According to Carson, "they never became dependent on buying and selling to make their living."

In other words, those Choctaw who began to embrace the economic opportunities of the early nineteenth century did not rush blindly into this exchange. Instead, they controlled the extent to which these economic relationships affected their lives.

One of the most noticeable agricultural innovations was the adoption of cattle as part of a livestock economy. Domesticated animals were not new to the Choctaw. Pigs and horses had been a feature of the Choctaw landscape for nearly a century by the early 1800s. But cattle were a recent addition, and they soon became an invaluable part of Choctaw involvement in the economy of the lower Mississippi Valley. By the 1820s, Choctaw men and women raised cattle, pigs, and horses for sale as well as for personal use. To provide more room and grazing for their livestock, more and more families began to move out of the villages.

In conjunction with many of their American neighbors in the Southeast, the Choctaw also started to cultivate cotton in the early nineteenth century. Because women were responsible for farming, they took the lead in bringing this new crop into the Choctaw world. Federal officials encouraged this transition, and in 1800, the Choctaw agent Samuel Mitchell gave out cotton seeds and lessons in their cultivation. The gardens that once held only corn, melons, beans, and other edible produce soon contained patches of cotton. The cotton grown in these gardens then became cloth on the spinning wheels and looms now present in many Choctaw homes.

Yet the introduction of cotton also brought the institution of slavery into Choctaw society. Because women were supposed to be the farmers, it was considered inappropriate for men to cultivate the land. Consequently, some of the wealthier men who saw the value of growing cotton chose to purchase African slaves to work in their fields. As of 1830, only 54 Choctaw out of a population of more than 17,000 owned slaves. Those Choctaw who owned slaves were therefore not representative of the entire community. Yet the presence of and acceptance of slavery reflected an important addition to both the Choctaw economy and Choctaw society.

The early-nineteenth-century Choctaw economy was built on new opportunities regulated by the customs of traditional Choctaw society. Cattle herds were both important and minimal additions to the preexisting livestock populations in Choctaw villages. Women who sold cloth woven from the cotton they grew in their gardens simply expanded the reach of their productive responsibilities. Choctaw men who purchased slaves to work in the fields abided by the gender roles of their culture.

MISSIONARIES AND THE CHOCTAW

In the late eighteenth and early nineteenth centuries, Choctaw political and economic life experienced gradual if not dramatic transformations because of increased interaction with Euro-Americans. But the scope of change went beyond those boundaries. The work of Christian missionaries also had an impact on Choctaw life in the first decades of the 1800s. These religious men and women came to the Choctaw as representatives of their denominations and the federal government. Missionaries sought to convert the American Indians to a life guided by Christian and American principles. Although the Choctaw did not accept the message in its entirety, they usually welcomed the messengers. As a result, Christian missionaries became an important part of Choctaw society in the early nineteenth century.

The first missionaries to the Choctaw arrived in 1818 through the support of the American Board of Commissions for Foreign Missions (ABCFM). The ABCFM was an organization founded by Congregationalists and Baptists in 1810 with the goal of spreading Christianity throughout the world. The founding of the Choctaw mission came only one year after the organization had started working among the Cherokee. Cyrus Kingsbury and Mr. and Mrs. Loring S. Williams were the missionaries selected by the ABCFM to work with the Choctaw. They established their mission in the summer of 1818 in the Western District of Choctaw territory.

Kingsbury and the Williamses arrived in Choctaw territory confident in the power of God and their faith to transform the lives

The Choctaw embraced Christianity, seeing it as a way to get an education in the white man's way in order to deal with the changing world around them. The Choctaw invited missionaries, like the one in this painting, to teach their children how to read the Bible, write, and do mathematics. By the early nineteenth century, there were Christian churches and schools throughout the Choctaw territory.

of the Choctaw. They were intent on introducing the Choctaw to the Bible but also believed in the need to promote the arts of civilization. In this manner, the missionaries were both agents of their religion and of the government. In 1819, in fact, Congress passed what was called the Civilization Fund Act. This piece of legislation set aside $10,000 annually to support the work of Christian missionaries among the American Indians.

The Choctaw welcomed the presence of these missionaries. Pushmataha, chief of the Southern towns, and Puckshunubbee, chief of the Western Division, each contributed several hundred dollars to support the missionaries' efforts. These and other financial contributions allowed the ABCFM to open other missions in Choctaw territory in the 1820s. By 1831, the Choctaw had provided nearly half of the funds necessary to meet the operating costs of the Christian missions in their territory.

But where the missionaries had multiple objectives, the Choctaw welcomed them with one thought in mind. They wanted their children to benefit from the instruction in missionary schools. To prepare their people for the changing world around them, Choctaw leaders, elders, and parents all believed it was necessary for their children to learn to read and write. They were less pleased, however, with the other aspects of the missionary presence. Parents criticized the missionaries for trying to turn their boys into farmers and did not like the strict discipline enforced in the schools. The Choctaw did their best to restrict the influence of the missionaries over their lives and the lives of their children.

In the late eighteenth and early nineteenth centuries, the Choctaw faced a rising power in the form of the United States. Their approach to handling the new nation was built on past experiences and cultural expectations. They sought to build a relationship with the Americans based on exchange and diplomacy. The Choctaw leadership even welcomed the possibility of cultural adaptation through the channel of missionary education for their children. By the 1820s, two things had become clear. First and foremost, the Choctaw were willing to adapt to changing conditions but were also intent on controlling the extent of those changes within their society. Second, the ability of the Choctaw to manage the intrusions of the United States and its citizens was growing weaker by the day.

Removal
and Division

In 1820, Choctaw delegates met with American treaty commissioners and signed the Treaty of Doak's Stand. That agreement gave the Choctaw millions of acres of land west of the Mississippi River but did not force them to relocate. Ten years later, the U.S. Senate ratified the Treaty of Dancing Rabbit Creek that set in motion the eventual removal of more than 12,000 Choctaw men, women, and children. Over the course of the 1820s, the overwhelming forces of American expansion and the damaging consequences of political infighting brought the Choctaw to a position they could never have imagined at the turn of the century. They were leaving the land of their origin for a new home west of the Mississippi River.

CHOCTAW POLITICS

Choctaw politics in the first three decades of the nineteenth century were defined by the rise of new leaders and ongoing efforts to develop stable relations with the United States. The Spanish were no longer a factor after the Treaty of San Lorenzo in 1795 and the Adams-Onís Treaty of 1819 collectively transferred Florida into American hands and finalized the border between U.S. and Spanish territory west of the Mississippi River. This meant that the Choctaw and other Southeastern Indians faced the Americans without the balancing influence of another European power. Choctaw diplomacy and politics had to adjust. These changing circumstances impacted both the nature of Choctaw leadership and the actions taken by Choctaw chiefs.

Historian Greg O'Brien has noted that the changes in political leadership among the Choctaw in the early nineteenth century were influenced by access to power. Most importantly, by the 1800s, the markers of success and authority were based on American principles and not Choctaw ones. "Increasingly," O'Brien states in his book *Choctaws in a Revolutionary Age*, "those who amassed great wealth dominated political decisions." In short, political authority in Choctaw society soon rested in fewer and fewer hands. Within a generation or two after the end of the American Revolution, those Choctaw men who chose to adopt aspects of American civilization were the ones who held most of the political power.

Many, though not all, of these rising leaders were men of mixed descent. They were the products of relationships between European male traders and Choctaw women that had grounded eighteenth-century alliances. Peter Pitchlynn, for example, was the grandson of an English trader and a Choctaw woman. His own father, John Pitchlynn, was a trader who served as an interpreter in all the Choctaw treaty councils between 1805 and 1830. Peter capitalized on his father's wealth and connections and by 1830 became a leading figure among the Choctaw. Other descendants of European traders rose to prominence as well. David Folsom was the son of Nathaniel Folsom, an Englishman who had two Choctaw wives and 24 children. Greenwood LeFlore's father, Louis, was a Canadian trader who married two Choctaw women of the Western Division to improve his business prospects. By the mid-1820s, David Folsom and Greenwood LeFlore signed Choctaw treaties and played important roles in Choctaw governance.

Nevertheless, while the descendants of traders gained influence, they did not control Choctaw politics. As of the 1820s, the three divisions were still led by Choctaw men without European heritage. In the past, scholars have asserted that mixed-descent individuals gained influence in the nineteenth century because they were more likely to welcome missions, schools, and other aspects of federal policy. Among the Choctaw, however, chiefs like Mushulatubbee retained power within the Eastern Division because they adapted well to the changing circumstances. Mushulatubbee owned 10 slaves and was a leading advocate of missionary schools. Indeed, the Choctaw chief's power in the Eastern Division was somewhat unmatched in the early nineteenth century because of the material wealth he had accumulated. Pushmataha, the chief of the Southern Division, was similarly positioned within Choctaw society.

Both the entrenched and rising leaders among the Choctaw shared a desire to construct a strong and peaceful relationship with the Americans. Some of the best examples of their efforts occurred in the 1810s, when both a militant Indian confederacy and the War of 1812 threatened American interests in the Southeast. In 1811, during his diplomatic visits to the Southeastern Indian tribes, the Shawnee leader Tecumseh held a council with the Choctaw. Tecumseh hoped to convince them to join the confederacy of tribes he and his brother Tenskwatawa, also called "the Prophet," had built in the Great Lakes region. But the Choctaw at this point had already decided that their best interests rested in a strong alliance with the United States. The leaders of all three Choctaw divisions rejected Tecumseh's requests.

Only two years later, a militant faction of Creek Indians calling themselves the Red Stick initiated what amounted to a civil war within the Creek confederacy. But when the violence of that

conflict spread beyond Creek territorial boundaries and threatened American settlements, the situation changed. The U.S. government sent soldiers to defeat the Creek, and Indian agent John
McKee suggested that the Choctaw receive gifts to remain neutral.

Chief Pushmataha was highly respected by Native Americans, Europeans,
and white Americans for his sharp wit, eloquent speaking style, and skills in
both war and diplomacy. He is thought of by many historians as the greatest
of all Choctaw chiefs.

Yet Pushmataha and other Choctaw leaders wanted no part of the Creek uprising. Instead, they offered the federal government the full military support of the Choctaw warriors.

Not only did Choctaw warriors ally with Americans in their war against the Creek, but they also served under General Andrew Jackson in the famous Battle of New Orleans. Both Jackson and the legislature of Mississippi Territory praised the efforts of the Choctaw. The Choctaw believed they had proved their worth to their non-Indian neighbors. It was an important step to building a relationship with the United States that they hoped would protect their territory and independence.

PRESSURE TO REMOVE

It would take more than the military efforts of Choctaw warriors and their leaders to satisfy American land hunger, however. From 1801 to 1820, the Choctaw signed treaties with the United States in which they ceded approximately 13 million acres (5.26 million ha) of land in present-day Alabama and Mississippi. Even these sizable cessions only increased American greed. In the first three decades of the nineteenth century, the non-Indian population of the region exploded. Such growth only strengthened the intentions of state officials to remove all American Indians living in Mississippi.

The five-year period after the end of the War of 1812 witnessed the most substantial population increase. From 1816 to 1820, the non-Indian population of Mississippi more than doubled, from just over 31,000 to nearly 75,000. Alabama, its eastern neighbor, recorded a population increase during that same period from 9,000 to more than 144,000. These incoming settlers wanted to grow cotton on the land claimed by the Choctaw. The rise of cotton as a cash crop and the fertile soil of Mississippi and Alabama thus fueled the hunger for land at both a local and state level. Shortly after Mississippi became a state in 1817, its elected officials pushed for the extinguishment of Indian land title.

Federal officials responded to these local and state interests. Secretary of War John C. Calhoun hoped to make an example of the Choctaw. If the Choctaw agreed to remove, it might encourage other tribes to relocate. At Calhoun's direction, three federal commissioners, including Andrew Jackson, met with Choctaw leaders in 1819. Jackson in particular believed that the Choctaw needed to move west of the Mississippi River for the good of both their people and the American citizens who would put the land to better use. The Choctaw rejected the commissioners' removal proposals with little hesitation. Pushmataha in particular made it clear that his people had no interest in leaving their land.

Pushmataha and the Choctaw had every reason to think that they would not have to move. The Choctaw had supported the American military efforts during the War of 1812, and they had welcomed the Christian missionaries who represented the federal government's civilization program. In 1816, after negotiating a treaty of friendship with the United States, the Choctaw had even received a promise that they would not be asked for any further land cessions.

Two critical factors undermined the Choctaw position. First, the state of Mississippi and the federal government would not give up their efforts to convince the Choctaw of the necessity of removal. Second, the Choctaw were not united in their resistance. The failure to secure Choctaw removal in 1819 created a wave of protest throughout the state of Mississippi. As a result, in 1820, Jackson received another federal appointment to negotiate a treaty with the Choctaw. Jackson and General Thomas Hinds were now charged with extinguishing the title to all Indian lands in Mississippi. Jackson was determined to succeed this time.

In the weeks leading up to the 1820 negotiations, there were signs that Jackson might be successful. First, a number of Choctaw believed that removal was either a good idea or inevitable. James Pitchlynn, the son of John and brother of Peter, was one of the former. He had written several letters to President James Monroe in 1819 claiming that a substantial number of Choctaw wanted to move west of the Mississippi River. There were also indications that some Choctaw leaders who were against a straight sale might be willing to exchange lands in Mississippi for land in the western territories.

The formal council began on October 10 after approximately 500 Choctaw had gathered at Doak's Stand, an open, grassy area on the Natchez road in Choctaw territory. Jackson opened negotiations by asserting that the Choctaw should remove peacefully before American settlers simply pushed them out of the way. To strengthen his proposal, he offered the Choctaw nearly 13 million acres (5.26 million ha) in the West in exchange for 5 million acres (2 million ha) of their Mississippi territory. The Choctaw remained somewhat resistant until Jackson threatened to revoke American friendship. On October 18, Mushulatubbee, Pushmataha, and other Choctaw leaders signed the Treaty of Doak's Stand.

The Choctaw only surrendered one-third of their land in Mississippi in the Treaty of Doak's Stand. Under the terms of the treaty, removal was a choice and not a necessity. Nevertheless, the agreement marked an important moment because of the foundation it laid for the treaties and relocations to come.

THE TREATY OF DANCING RABBIT CREEK

Three things changed for the Choctaw between 1820 and 1830. First, state and federal governments increased the pressure on the Choctaw to remove. Second, David Folsom, Greenwood LeFlore, and their supporters made dramatic moves to alter the Choctaw system of government. Third, the resulting discussions of removal and struggles for power fractured the Choctaw. All three of these elements ultimately led to the 1830 Treaty of Dancing Rabbit Creek that arranged for the removal of the Choctaw from Mississippi.

The Indian Removal Act passed by Congress in May 1830 had its origins in several decades of debate, discussion, and planning.

Thomas Jefferson had first expressed the possibility of relocating eastern Indians to land west of the Mississippi River after the Louisiana Purchase in 1803. The larger policy took shape over the next two decades, as illustrated by treaties like that negotiated with the Choctaw at Doak's Stand in 1820. But it finally became legislation during Andrew Jackson's first term as president. The Indian Removal Act gave Jackson the authority to offer western lands to those American Indian tribes who chose to relocate.

Although the Indian Removal Act presented at least a nominal choice, the state of Mississippi was more direct. In February 1829, Governor Gerard Brandon signed a law extending state jurisdiction over Choctaw lands. From that point forward, any Choctaw living in Mississippi would have to live under that state's laws. Through such actions, Mississippi and other southern states sought to undermine Indian sovereignty and make life extremely uncomfortable for the Creek, Choctaw, Chickasaw, and Cherokee. These states knew that President Jackson supported their approach.

Mississippi's assault on Choctaw sovereignty occurred even as the Choctaw political structure was undergoing a substantial transformation. In the spring of 1826, Mushulatubbee resigned his position as chief of the Eastern Division. His support of a treaty signed in 1825 and the growing influence of David Folsom had combined to weaken the chief's authority. Shortly thereafter, the warriors of the Western Division removed their chief and replaced him with Greenwood LeFlore. Then in August, Folsom and LeFlore brought their two divisions together to form a new government created by a new constitution. Two years later, the Southern Division of the Choctaw elected a chief named John Garland, who supported Folsom and LeFlore. According to Folsom, LeFlore, and Garland, all three Choctaw divisions now existed under a national government.

But even this new government found it difficult to match the state and federal powers arrayed against them. Disputes within the Choctaw Nation were just as problematic. Once Mississippi recognized that Jackson and the federal government would support its moves against the Choctaw, the state legislature pushed its jurisdiction even further. This increased pressure led Mushulatubbee and his supporters to conclude that removal might be a good idea after all. Just as important, LeFlore, Folsom, and Garland began to share that opinion. In one final transformation, and in order to be united in their dealings with the United States, Garland and Folsom resigned their positions so that the national council could elect LeFlore as the chief for all three Choctaw divisions.

The Choctaw Address Congress, 1825

In October 1824, a delegation of Choctaw traveled to Washington, D.C. This delegation included three prominent Choctaw chiefs, Mushulatubbee, Pushmataha, and Puckshunubbee. The trip was marred by tragedy before they reached Washington when Puckshunubbee died from injuries related to an accidental fall in Maysville, Kentucky.

Upon their arrival in Washington in early 1825, the Choctaw intended to obtain assistance from the federal government. Most importantly, they wanted the protection of the United States from its citizens so that the Choctaw could continue to adapt to the changing circumstances in peace and safety. The following is an excerpt from a letter presented by the delegation to Congress.

> We have but small tracts of territory remaining, and our numbers are comparatively few. The majority of those east of the Mississippi are turning their attention to agriculture, are settling themselves, and would in time become useful citizens. We admit, at the same time, that a large number still continue a wandering life, are wretched and

Rather than remain in Mississippi and submit to state law or resist through violent or legal means, LeFlore and the Choctaw government chose to propose a removal treaty. However, LeFlore had competition in the person of Mushulatubbee and his supporters. President Jackson could seemingly pick which Choctaw leaders he would talk to about removal. To prevent this possibility, LeFlore used military force to intimidate Mushulatubbee. But it was not that simple. When two federal commissioners arrived in Choctaw territory in September 1830, the subsequent treaty

degraded. These it would give us pleasure to see settled west of the Mississippi. It would be better for them, and better for those that remained. But you cannot persuade all to remove. The gradual operation of the laws which you may enact with regard to this subject would probably effect much. But there are those whom the strongest inducements could scarcely persuade to leave the land which contains the bones of their fathers, and which has been rendered dear to them by the recollections of youth. The important question then presents itself, What will you do with those that remain? What measures will you adopt to improve their condition, to promote their happiness? It is this great point to which our address is intended principally to direct your attention.

As connected with the subject and with the question just proposed, we are constrained to say that in several of the southern States we are denied privileges to which, as members of the human family, we are of right entitled. However qualified by education we may be, we are neither permitted to hold offices, nor to give our testimony in courts of justice, although our dearest rights may be at stake. Can this be a correct policy? Is it just? Is it humane?

councils encompassed men and women from all three Choctaw divisions, not just LeFlore and the national council.

The final treaty, however, was not worked out in those larger meetings. Records of the council sessions demonstrate strong resistance to removal among the Choctaw delegates, especially the women. Seven elder Choctaw women were present at the council meetings, and they sat in the center of the circle formed by the male Choctaw in attendance. Land fell under the purview of their female authority, and they refused to allow the men to cede territory. One of the women even threatened to cut one of the Choctaw men with a butcher knife when he expressed a willingness to surrender the land. But federal officials bypassed that resistance by holding a smaller council with a select group of leaders several days after the official sessions had ended. LeFlore, Folsom, and Mushulatubbee were among those who signed what became known as the Treaty of Dancing Rabbit Creek. The agreement ceded all 10 million acres (4 million ha) of land remaining in Choctaw hands in Mississippi. Each Choctaw would be given a choice. He or she could relocate to the West or remain in Mississippi, receive an allotment of land, and become an American citizen.

REMOVING AND REMAINING

Most Choctaw responded to the news of the Treaty of Dancing Rabbit Creek with outrage. Members of all three divisions moved to replace the chiefs who had signed the agreement and betrayed the wishes of their people. Many Choctaw rightly charged that their leading men had received substantial financial benefits for signing a treaty of dispossession. But the anger that led to the

---

(Opposite map) During the Trails of Tears, members of the Cherokee, Choctaw, Chickasaw, Creek, and Seminole tribes were moved from their home territories and relocated to Indian Territory (present-day Oklahoma). In 1830, the Choctaw were the first to be removed. Hundreds died on the way to their destinations.

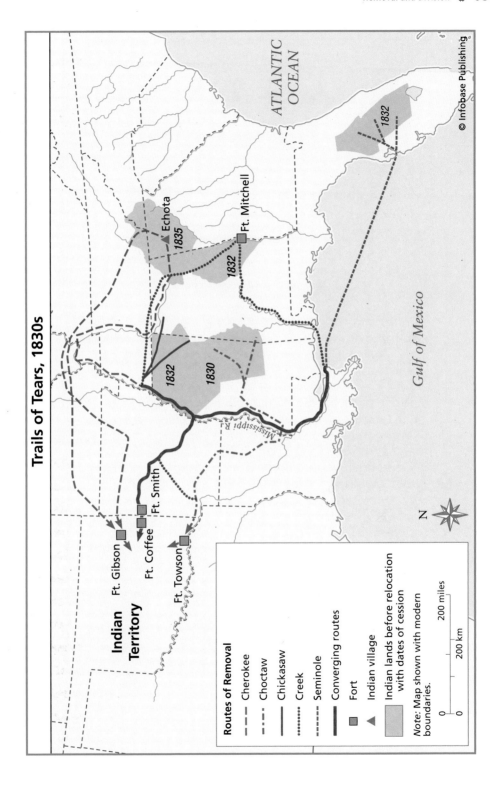

Trails of Tears, 1830s

Ft. Mitchell

Echota
1835

1832

1832

1832

1830

Mississippi R.

Ft. Smith

Ft. Gibson

Ft. Coffee

Ft. Towson

Indian Territory

ATLANTIC OCEAN

Gulf of Mexico

N

Routes of Removal

- - - - Cherokee
- · - · - Choctaw
———— Chickasaw
·········· Creek
- - - - Seminole
━━━━ Converging routes

■ Fort
▲ Indian village

Indian lands before relocation with dates of cession

Note: Map shown with modern boundaries.

0   200 miles
0   200 km

© Infobase Publishing

ACTS

OF THE

STATE OF GEORGIA

AN ACT

To ratify and confirm certain articles of agreement and cession entered into on the 24th day of April 1802, between the Commissioners of the State of Georgia on the one part, and the Commissioners of the United States on the other part.

WHEREAS the Commissioners of the State of Georgia, to wit: James Jackson, Abraham Baldwin, and John Milledge, duly authorized and appointed by, and on the part and behalf of the said State of Georgia; and the Commissioners of the United States, James Madison, Albert Gallatin, and Levi Lincoln, duly authorized and appointed by, and on the part and behalf of the said United States, to make an amicable settlement of limits, between the two Sovereignties, after a due examination of their respective powers, did, on the 24th day of April last, enter into a deed of articles, and mutual cession, in the words following, to wit:

ARTICLES of agreement and cession, entered into on the twenty-fourth day of April, one thousand eight hundred and two, between the Commissioners appointed on the part of the United States, by virtue of an act entitled, " An act for an amicable settlement of limits

Despite Supreme Court Chief Justice John Marshall's ruling in *Worcester v. Georgia* that the Cherokee retained certain rights in their own lands, Indian removal became an official government policy of the United States. The agreement above documents the forced removal of the indigenous peoples from their homeland in Georgia on April 24, 1831.

ouster of LeFlore and others could not alter the terms of the 1830 treaty.

Enforcement was complicated. The fourteenth article and the opinions of Indian agent William Ward disrupted the choice presented by the treaty. That article contained the provision allowing any Choctaw to remain in Mississippi and become an American citizen. Ward, however, wanted the Choctaw out of Mississippi and adamantly refused to allow any Choctaw to take advantage of this provision. His defiance meant that those Choctaw who wanted to stay in Mississippi were left in limbo. If they stayed, they did so without any means of federal support.

In the meantime, federal officials made plans for those Choctaw who favored removal. From the end of 1830 to 1833, nearly 13,000 Choctaw left Mississippi and made their way west. The first party of approximately 1,000 left in December 1830, only a couple of months after the treaty was signed. By all accounts, they hoped to move west first in order to secure the best land in their new home. Their early removal also allowed them to avoid the invasion of Choctaw lands that followed the announcement of the treaty.

As of the fall of 1831, the federal government had established a plan for the removal of the Choctaw over the next several years. The first stage would oversee the relocation of 6,000, or about a third of the total Choctaw population. In the end, only 4,000 took part in a journey plagued by poor food, miserable weather, and death. At least 250 died, and most of those who completed the removal suffered from exhaustion and sickness when it ended. The second stage of the removal plan included nearly 6,000 Choctaw in the fall of 1832. In addition to poor weather, the different removal parties encountered a cholera epidemic sweeping through the Mississippi River valley. Although it is difficult to be exact, once again at least several hundred Choctaw died during the journey.

The last of the three government-organized removal parties left Mississippi in October 1833 and arrived in the western territories in late December. A combination of water and land travel made their relocation more efficient than those of previous years.

Nevertheless, the journey still brought misery and death. Once they arrived, it meant that approximately 12,500 Choctaw had now settled west of the Mississippi River. It also meant that as of early 1834, nearly 7,000 Choctaw remained in Mississippi. Most of those assumed they would live under the protection of the fourteenth article of the Treaty of Dancing Rabbit Creek. They were wrong.

THE TREATY DIVIDES THE CHOCTAW

The Treaty of Dancing Rabbit Creek was both a product of and a catalyst for the division of the Choctaw. External pressure for removal at the local, state, and federal level in the 1820s made it difficult for the Choctaw to resist, and political infighting further weakened their position. But the 1830 treaty created an even more substantial split within the larger Choctaw community.

"We were told as kids," the character Delores Love explains in *Shell Shaker*, "that before the Choctaws left Mississippi, they came here and grabbed a little bit of Nanih Waiya to take with them on the long walk." For the first time since its birth in the seventeenth century, the majority of the Choctaw confederacy would live far from that sacred site. And from the 1830s on, the distance between Mississippi and Choctaw territory in the West, not just politics, would separate members of that community.

The Post-removal Choctaw Republic

B y the late 1830s, the removal of the Choctaw from Mississippi was nearly complete. More than 12,000 men, women, and children now had to adapt to life in a new environment. Their successful recovery is a testament to the strength of their community, but the ongoing pressures they faced were also evidence of the persistence of American expansion. The removal of the 1830s did not isolate the Choctaw from the voracious land hunger of the United States for long. By the end of the nineteenth century, the Choctaw would be on the verge of once again losing all that they had retained.

AFTER REMOVAL

Removal from Mississippi was devastating. Those who survived the journey now had to rebuild their lives in what Choctaw scholar Donna Akers refers to as a "land of death." Despite the obstacles they faced, however, the Choctaw gradually found a way to prosper. They were the first of the southeastern tribes to move west of the Mississippi River under the terms of the Indian Removal Act. And their treaties had provided the Choctaw with some of the best agricultural land in what the U.S. government designated in 1834 as Indian Territory. The Choctaw lands were specifically located within the present-day state of Oklahoma, though Indian Territory encompassed all American lands west of the Mississippi River exclusive of Missouri, Louisiana, and Arkansas Territory.

Because the Choctaw removal occurred over the course of more than three years, many individuals and families had the ability to prepare for the journey. Consequently, a few prominent Choctaw like the Pitchlynns were able to relocate with a substantial amount of their property. As they established a new home in Indian Territory, they did so with the livestock, slaves, and farming implements they had brought with them from Mississippi. With this property in tow, they hoped to recreate the comfortable lifestyle they had enjoyed east of the Mississippi River. Men like Peter Pitchlynn also served as the commercial mediators for the larger community, buying goods from American traders to sell for a profit in Choctaw territory.

Although wealthier families like the Pitchlynns maintained larger farms and herds of livestock, most of the Choctaw maintained modest farms once they recovered from removal and found a place to settle. Interviews conducted in the 1930s with Choctaw men and women contain frequent references to the relatively small plots of land their parents and grandparents maintained during the nineteenth century. In all cases, these interviews demonstrate that the Choctaw women continued to be responsible for the cultivation of the land. They oversaw the four or five acres (1.6 or 2 ha) of corn, potatoes, and other crops necessary to feed their families. In addition, the average Choctaw family may have had a few oxen and up to a dozen cattle to add to their subsistence. These farms tended to be spread throughout the territory, which meant that the Choctaw did not live in compact villages like they had in Mississippi.

Peter Pitchlynn was a mixed-race chief of Choctaw and Anglo-American descent. Pitchlynn, knowledgeable in both American and Choctaw traditions, became principal chief of the Choctaw after the tribe had been removed to Indian Territory.

The post-removal experience was about more than establishing new homes, however. The Choctaw also sought to build or rebuild the social, political, and economic structures necessary for the successful growth and survival of their community. They quickly constructed churches and schools. Over time, they also established new relationships with the Chickasaw, who had also suffered removal in the 1830s.

The Choctaw government in Indian Territory was initially a continuation of that which had been established in the written constitution of 1826. That constitution was revised in 1834, but its foundation remained intact. The three divisions still existed and maintained their own leaders, but each division sent representatives to a national legislature. Over the next 20 years, however, Choctaw governance underwent a series of significant alterations. In 1837, the Choctaw agreed to share their land in Indian Territory with the Chickasaw. According to this agreement, the Chickasaw would be a separate political division and would hold joint title to the land. In part because of the problems created by this shared governance, the Choctaw signed a treaty with the United States in 1855 that drew a boundary line between the Chickasaw and Choctaw lands. Five years later, an ongoing power struggle among influential men in the nation led the Choctaw to revise their constitution. The government created under this document had at its foundation the elected district chiefs. It also, however, established the office of principal chief of the Choctaw Nation. What some Choctaw had hoped to establish in the 1820s had now become official.

In the midst of these significant changes, most of the Choctaw maintained critical elements of their culture. Choctaw historian Clara Sue Kidwell asserts in her book *The Choctaws in Oklahoma* that "Choctaw cultural identity was still largely intact in two of its most important indicators, language and kinship systems." Although more and more Choctaw knew English, the Choctaw language retained a firm hold in daily interactions. And while aspects of social relations and gender roles had changed to an extent, the core elements of Choctaw culture had not. Even traditional pastimes like the ballgames witnessed by American artist George Catlin in 1838 testified to the maintenance of some of these common practices.

Overall, the decades after removal displayed an equal measure of disruption and continuity in the lives of Choctaw men, women, and children. On the one hand, removal had displaced them from the land of their origin. The sacred ground of Nanih Waiya and the homes they had built over the course of the seventeenth and eighteenth centuries were now in the hands of American citizens. It was a severe upheaval whose impact can never truly be expressed in words. Yet the lives of the Choctaw in Indian Territory also displayed important expressions of continuity and persistence. Women were still responsible for the farms, and young boys learned to hunt at a young age. Even as they negotiated a new relationship with the United States and its citizens, the Choctaw did not abandon the heart of their cultural and political identity.

THE CHOCTAW AND THE CIVIL WAR

Despite the dislocation caused by the removal of the early 1830s, the Choctaw had managed to rebuild their lives over the course of several decades. But the Choctaw and their neighbors, like the United States as a whole, could not escape the national crisis known as the Civil War. The secession of South Carolina from the Union in December 1860 after the election of Abraham Lincoln triggered the formation of the Confederate States of America, and the attack on Fort Sumter in April 1861 provided the final spark for war. Indian Territory shared a border with the seceded states of Texas and Arkansas. In addition, the Confederate States of America sent diplomats to negotiate an alliance with the Cherokee, Chickasaw, Creek, and Choctaw in early 1861. The Choctaw would have to decide which side they would join. They would not be allowed to remain neutral.

It might seem strange that the Choctaw chose to ally with the Confederacy. In doing so, they not only broke their relationship with the federal government but also sided with the new nation that included the very people who had taken their lands in Mississippi. The Choctaw decision, however, makes sense when viewed

Catlin's Description of a Choctaw Ballgame

In the 1830s, American painter George Catlin was able to observe a ballgame similar to modern lacrosse. He painted several portraits of the game, including this one called *Ball Play of the Choctaw—Ball Up* (1834).

In the early 1830s, American painter George Catlin made several trips west of the Mississippi River to observe and capture on canvas the lives of American Indians. On one of those trips, he visited the Choctaw, who had only recently been removed from Mississippi. During his visit, Catlin painted portraits of Mushulatubbee and Peter Pitchlynn.

The American painter was also fortunate enough to observe a traditional Choctaw ballgame, which was an important pastime. He painted several images of the game itself and painted a portrait of Tullockchishko, the most renowned Choctaw ballplayer of the time. The following is an excerpt of a long description of the Choctaw ballgame Catlin observed.

During the afternoon, we loitered about amongst the different tents and shantees of the two encampments, and afterwards, at sundown, witnessed the ceremony of measuring out the ground, and erecting the "byes" or goals which were to guide the play. Each party had their goal made with two upright posts, about 25 feet high and six feet apart, set firm in the ground, with a pole across the top. These goals were about forty or fifty rods apart; and at a point just half way between, was another small stake, driven down, where the ball was to be thrown up at the firing of a gun, to be struggled for by the players.

All this preparation was made by some old men, who were, it seems, selected to be the judges of the play, who drew a line from one bye to the other; to which directly came from the woods, on both sides, a great concourse of women and old men, boys and girls, and dogs and horses, where bets were to be made on the play . . . when at length the game commenced, by the judges throwing up the ball at the firing of a gun; when an instant struggle ensued between the players, who were some six or seven hundred in numbers, and were mutually endeavoring to catch the ball in their sticks, and throw it home and between their respective stakes; which, whenever successfully done, counts for one game . . . each time the ball was passed between the stakes of either party, one was counted for their game, and a halt of about one minute; when it was again started by the judges of the play, and a similar struggle ensued; and so on until the successful party arrived at 100, which was the limit of the game.

in a larger context. First, the federal government pulled its troops out of Indian Territory early in 1861, thus abandoning its treaty obligations to the Choctaw, Chickasaw, and other Indian nations. Second, in May of 1861, Confederate soldiers captured Fort Smith on the border of Arkansas and Indian Territory and cut off Indian Territory from the Union. Third, those Choctaw who were slaveholders already shared the interests of the Confederacy. Fourth and finally, the treaty they signed with the Confederacy resolved to guarantee the Choctaw ownership of their land forever.

Over the course of four years, Indian Territory and its residents suffered tremendously from a combination of violence and indifference. The Confederacy never provided the full protection it had promised. While the eastern seaboard served as the most prominent theater in the war, Indian Territory did not escape the bloodshed. By the end of 1861, Choctaw warriors were officially enlisted in and fighting for the Confederate army. More than 1,000 Choctaw men continued to fight for the declining cause of the secessionists until the early months of 1865. Fortunately for the Choctaw in Indian Territory, the war did not bring the physical devastation it brought to the Creek and Cherokee. No significant battles were fought on their lands, and they did not experience the internal disputes of their Native neighbors.

When the war ended, however, the Choctaw had to come to terms with a U.S. government that had been their declared enemy for the past four years. At the end of April 1866, more than a year after the end of the Civil War, Choctaw and Chickasaw delegates signed a treaty with the United States. Known simply as the Treaty of 1866, this agreement included a total of 51 separate articles that encompassed everything from the construction of post offices to the salary of interpreters. It also reestablished peaceful relations between the Choctaw and the United States and granted amnesty for any and all "past offenses" by the Choctaw against the laws of the United States. Most importantly, however, the federal government viewed and treated the Choctaw as a defeated nation.

The Treaty of 1866 also confirmed that from that point forward, the Choctaw, like the United States as a whole, could no longer permit involuntary servitude or slavery. In addition, the African American men and women freed under this provision would have to be treated with equality under Choctaw law. The treatment of freedmen went beyond legal conditions. The treaty declared that "they shall be entitled to as much land as they may cultivate for the support of themselves and families." Under these terms, then, the Choctaw would have to accept the former slaves as part of their community.

The Civil War was a traumatic event for the Choctaw. In the end, however, it was not as damaging as it could have been. As of 1866, the Choctaw maintained control over their territory and their community. Even the physical impact of the war had not undermined the relative prosperity the Choctaw enjoyed in the aftermath of removal. But once the war was over, the next struggle began.

LEGACIES OF THE TREATY OF 1866

The Treaty of 1866 reestablished peaceful relations between the Choctaw and the United States. Still, while the violence of the Civil War had ended, an even bigger fight loomed. The U.S. government wanted to make Indian Territory into a state and hoped to turn its Indian residents into assimilated members of society. The Choctaw and their neighbors had their own ideas. For much of the late nineteenth century, they fought to maintain the integrity of their territory and political institutions.

Plans for the advancement of Indian Territory into a state in the Union began with the federal government's proposals in the Treaty of 1866. The eighth article of that agreement laid out the steps necessary to create a General Council for Indian Territory. This council would consist of delegates from each tribe in the territory and would have the authority to legislate in matters related to intertribal affairs, common defense, internal improvements, and criminal justice. The Department of the Interior would provide oversight as the infrastructure of this territorial government developed. It would be the first step toward an application for statehood.

As implied by this article, the federal government had similar plans written into the treaties signed with the other tribes in Indian Territory after the Civil War. Although the tribes did not initially have an interest in creating such a council, they took action when it appeared that Congress might move to impose a territorial government upon them. In 1870, representatives from numerous tribes, including the Choctaw, met to discuss their response. The result of these meetings was an agreement known as the Okmulgee Constitution. Although this pact demonstrated the American Indians' willingness to create a government for Indian Territory, it also displayed clear resistance to the proposals made by the federal government. The Choctaw voted in favor of the Okmulgee Constitution in October 1871. In so doing, they expressed their support for the political autonomy of tribes in Indian Territory, the preservation of their lands, and the opposition to any government imposed by Congress.

The position taken by the Choctaw was a crucial demonstration of their belief in the sovereignty of their nation. But this political battle was not their only problem. The sixth article of the Treaty of 1866 gave permission to companies approved by the U.S. government to lay tracks for railroads through Choctaw and Chickasaw lands. This single article had a tremendous impact in the decades that followed.

The treaty granted the right of way to railroad companies. But more than just land for the actual railroad tracks would be involved in the process. The sixth article also stated that the Choctaw could buy stock in the railroad company using sections of their land instead of cash. This gave both the railroads and the federal government an opening and a reason to push for the sale of Choctaw land. The railroads wanted the land to subsidize construction, and the government wanted to encourage the Choctaw to break up the larger reservation through land sales.

Treaties made with the Choctaw and other western tribes made huge amounts of land on the Great Plains available to the public. This paved the way for railroad construction to go right through Native American homelands.

This focus on the land was a part of both the 1866 treaty specifically and late-nineteenth-century federal policy in general. The eleventh article of the treaty presented the possibility of the allotment of Choctaw territory. In short, the land would be divided up and distributed among the Choctaw in smaller sections. No longer would the land be held in common by the entire tribe. This proposal was part of the larger push for the assimilation of Indians into American society by turning them into private landowners. Allotment was proposed in numerous treaties in the nineteenth century before becoming the official policy of the federal government in the General Allotment Act of 1887. It was one more federal policy the Choctaw resisted.

In their approach to both the railroad and allotment, the Choctaw sought to maintain the unity of their territory and their government. It would not be easy. Even as the United States sought to turn Indian Territory into a state, it had begun to take a more aggressive stance against the sovereignty of Indian nations. In 1871, Congress officially ended the policy of negotiating treaties with Indian tribes. Under this new policy, the federal government would no longer recognize Indian tribes as sovereign. Instead, they would be considered wards of the government.

The Choctaw therefore confronted an array of forces in the late nineteenth century. The Treaty of 1866 had given them the right to choose whether or not they would provide land to the railroads, and the Choctaw held tight to that choice. But in 1882, Congress passed a law that gave the federal government the right of eminent domain over all of Indian Territory. Choctaw resistance had been undermined yet again by the impositions of the U.S. government. By the late 1880s, the railroads had begun to move into Choctaw Territory in the southeastern corner of present-day Oklahoma.

The arrival of the railroads brought more than modern transportation to the region. It also signaled the arrival of railroad men. Many of these men were bachelors who viewed marriage to a Choctaw woman as one way to gain access to the rights and privileges of tribal membership. This membership provided access to the land and its resources. Indeed, white men who married Choctaw women were responsible for opening coal mines on Choctaw lands in the 1870s and granting leases to railroad companies in the 1890s. Through marriage, these men were also able to evade the numerous attempts of the Choctaw General Council to regulate the presence of non-Indians in the Choctaw Nation.

Between the end of the Civil War and the end of the nineteenth century, the Choctaw struggled against an overwhelming assortment of federal, local, and business interests. In the 1890s, however, they faced one of the more dangerous assaults through the policy of allotment. The Choctaw had repeatedly resisted attempts by the federal government to end their practice of owning the land as a community and not as individuals. But in 1897, they believed they had no choice but to submit to the demands of the federal government and signed what was known as the Atoka Agreement. This agreement, ratified by Congress in 1898, established a plan for the allotment of Choctaw lands. In addition to allotment, this agreement also initiated a critical process that granted the extension of federal authority over their lands in terms of legal and criminal jurisdiction as well. As of March 4, 1906, the sovereign Choctaw government would cease to exist.

Over a period of nearly 70 years, the Choctaw endured a series of tremendous highs and lows. Despite all of the obstacles in their path, most Choctaw had been able to recover from the trauma of removal and rebuild their lives in a new home. The relative prosperity of this recovery was then interrupted by war. Yet the violent assaults of the Civil War were not the worst the Choctaw would face in the nineteenth century. In combination, the American government and its citizens sought to gain a foothold in Indian Territory by gaining access to and control of the land and its resources. By the end of the nineteenth century, it appeared that this goal had been accomplished.

The Choctaw in the Twentieth Century

In the twentieth century, struggles over power, land, and culture defined the experience of the Choctaw Nation in Oklahoma. In many ways this was nothing new. The federal government simply continued its efforts to assimilate American Indians and undermine tribal relationships. American citizens moving into the region added to this pressure. They wanted the territory to become a state, and they wanted to gain access to the natural resources located on Choctaw lands. Yet, as one example of the larger successes of American Indians in the United States during that 100-year period, the Choctaw did more than just survive these troubles. In fact, the Choctaw were stronger at the end of the century than they had been at the beginning of it.

CITIZENSHIP AND STATEHOOD

The continued existence of the Choctaw Nation was by no means assured based on events at the turn of the century. The allotment of Choctaw territory under the Atoka Agreement of 1898 not only divided the lands held in common and established a process that would terminate the sovereign Choctaw government, but it also initiated a debate over Choctaw and American citizenship and laid the foundation for the state of Oklahoma. All of these matters were of utmost concern to the Choctaw in the first decades of the twentieth century.

In 1893, the federal government created what was known as the Dawes Commission. The primary mission of this small group of presidential appointees was to convince the Cherokee, Choctaw, Creek, Chickasaw, and Seminole to accept allotment. But the scope of its authority soon widened. In 1896, the U.S. Congress authorized the Dawes Commission to decide who was or was not a member of the Choctaw tribe. The commission categorized applicants as Citizens by Blood, Citizens by Marriage, Minor Citizens by Blood, New Born Citizens by Blood, Freedmen (African Americans formerly enslaved by tribal members), New Born Freedmen, and Minor Freedmen. This policy was a direct attack on the sovereign authority of the Choctaw government. As a result, the issue of citizenship became a battle for power between the United States and the Choctaw. By 1900, the Dawes Commission had added more than 2,000 men and women to the Choctaw tribal rolls. Principal chief Green McCurtain and the Choctaw General Council pledged to oppose these new additions. For several decades, the Choctaw government had controlled the citizenship rights of white men who married Choctaw women and recently emigrated Mississippi Choctaw. They did not welcome the interference of the federal government in these matters.

The legal resistance of the Choctaw government resulted in what was known as the Supplementary Agreement of 1902. This document did not bring peace to the Choctaw Nation. It set a limit on land distributed per allotment, created a court for hearing citizenship disputes, and established a deadline for the enrollment of Mississippi Choctaw in the Choctaw Nation. But it also played a role in an extremely contentious election among the Choctaw

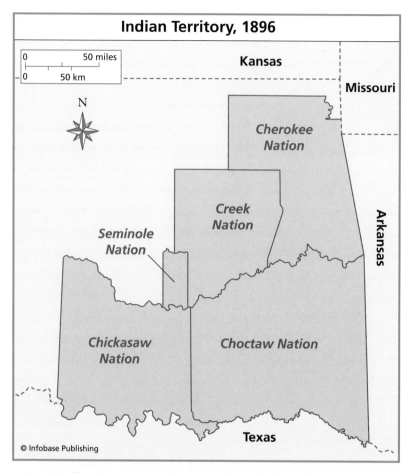

In 1893, the Dawes Commission carved up tribal land into plots that were then divided among members of the Cherokee, Chickasaw, Creek, Seminole, and Choctaw tribes. In 1896, the commission was given the authority to accept or reject applicants for tribal membership based on whether the tribal government had previously recognized the applicant as a member of the tribe and other legal requirements.

in 1902. At one point, it appeared that three different chiefs had been elected as the Choctaw struggled to decide whether to resist further or accept the policy of allotment and federal power. Once Green McCurtain was finally confirmed as chief, the situation appeared settled. He would preside over the final years of the sovereign Choctaw Nation.

The end of the Choctaw government was intended to coincide with the statehood of Oklahoma. Yet Native Americans in the region had other plans. The fourth article of the Treaty of Dancing Rabbit Creek stated both that "no Territory or state shall ever have a right to pass laws for the government of the Choctaw Nation of Red People and their descendants," and that "no part of the land granted them shall ever be embraced in any Territory or State." Chief McCurtain focused on that principle and attempted to unite the Cherokee, Creek, and other tribes against statehood as early as 1902. McCurtain proposed that Indian Territory join the Union as a separate state named Sequoyah instead of joining with Oklahoma Territory. Despite these efforts, the federal government's decision to push for combined statehood could not be stopped.

Oklahoma officially became the forty-sixth state on November 16, 1907. The separate entities known as Indian Territory and Oklahoma Territory were now one. No longer would Indian Territory exist outside of the Union. Instead, the American Indian and white residents of the region would now live under the same political institution. This union would not be smooth.

CHOCTAW LAND IN OKLAHOMA

Oklahoma statehood contradicted the terms of the Treaty of Dancing Rabbit Creek. It also brought the resources of Choctaw lands closer to the hands of American citizens and private business interests. Statehood proved to be more than just a political imposition. It also had a critical economic impact on the Choctaw Nation and its citizens.

Less than a year after Oklahoma became a state, the U.S. Congress passed a law altering prior restrictions on Choctaw lands. Under the allotment policy established by the Atoka Agreement, it was not possible for Choctaw landowners to sell their allotments until after a 25-year trust period had passed. The idea was that Choctaw men and women needed that time to gain a full understanding of private land ownership and its implications. The 1908 congressional policy eliminated that trust period for all whites married to Choctaw women, all freedmen, and any person who had less than one-half degree of Choctaw blood. Some restrictions were lifted for those of mixed descent above one-half degree of Choctaw blood. In the end, only full-blood Choctaw were not allowed to sell their land.

This policy shift had immediate consequences. Nearly 16,000 residents of the Choctaw Nation now had the ability to sell their land. That number included the almost 6,000 freedmen who resided on tribal lands. In addition, the lifted restrictions meant that the Choctaw and freedmen held patents to their land. The state of Oklahoma argued that this land was therefore subject to state property taxes. Any taxation had the potential to cause further land loss among the Choctaw. Only a ruling by the U.S. Supreme Court in the case of *Choate v. Trapp* stopped state officials from taxing Choctaw lands.

Despite this substantial legal victory, Choctaw land and the resources on that land remained under attack for the first three decades of the twentieth century. Guardians appointed by state courts mismanaged the allotments granted to Choctaw minors and orphans. In addition, American businesses had their sights set on gaining access to the coal and timber resources located on Choctaw lands. These assets were extremely valuable. A 1909 report estimated that the Choctaw lands encompassed $12 million worth of coal and nearly $2 million worth of timber. Both coal and timber were particularly important to the American railroad industry, which meant that there was a ready market for these goods in the late nineteenth and early twentieth centuries. Although the oil discoveries of the 1920s hurt the market for coal, the Choctaw eventually sold their coal and asphalt stores for a total of $8.5 million in 1948.

Hardwood forests made up a substantial portion of the southeastern segment of Choctaw territory west of the Mississippi. By the late 1800s, the timber had also become a target for railroads and other outside businesses hoping to profit from accessible resources. This timber consequently rested at the heart of the allotment battles of the early twentieth century. Despite the protests of Chief McCurtain and others, the Department of the Interior allowed the timberlands to be allotted. By the 1920s, most of the timberlands had been sold at public auction. For the remainder of the 1900s and into the 2000s, the timber industry profited from wood harvested on those lands even as the Choctaw received little compensation.

Yet even as these actions taken to harvest the natural resources on Choctaw lands represented an attack, the ways in which the events played out also led to a measure of continuity. Clara Sue Kidwell has even asserted that per capita payments from coal sales and other deals were critical elements of Choctaw continuity. The promise of such payments, she writes, "kept the hopes of a new generation of Choctaws alive and perpetuated its awareness of its Choctaw identity." In other words, in order to make the per capita payments, the federal government and the Choctaw had to keep track of membership and land ownership. In its own way, this process maintained connections within the Choctaw community.

Allotment and mineral leases combined to decimate the landholdings of the Choctaw over the course of the first half of the twentieth century. In this respect, the Choctaw were like almost every other Indian tribe in the United States during the same period. By the 1950s, only approximately 16,000 acres (6,475 ha) of Choctaw lands remained unallotted. That is all that remained of the approximately 15 million acres (6 million ha) of communal land gained by the Choctaw in the Treaty of Dancing Rabbit Creek. Yet not all the consequences of these attacks were negative, as parts of the process required a record of Choctaw membership.

CHOCTAW INDIAN COUNTRY

Economic concerns and federal policies played influential roles throughout the twentieth century in relation to the continuation of the Choctaw. Yet, as had been the case for several hundred years, economics and politics did not define Choctaw identity. Despite the ongoing assaults against Choctaw sovereignty, lands, and culture, Choctaw men, women, and children continued to practice and maintain important aspects of their traditional way of life. Though American policy and society did not make it easy, the members of the Choctaw Nation were still very much Choctaw at the end of the twentieth century.

There are a number of ways to illustrate the continued strength of Choctaw identity in the twentieth century. Even a brief look at

Although Choctaw people adapted long ago to modern ways, Choctaw traditions continue to be a vital aspect of community life. Each generation teaches the next about social dance, beadwork, stickball, basket patterns, and other elements of what it means to be Choctaw.

the Web site for the Choctaw Nation of Oklahoma reveals the continued importance of several aspects of their culture. The School of Choctaw Language offers classes for high school and college students as well as online materials to bolster the ongoing education of its members. Links to traditional food recipes and clothing provide access to other elements of Choctaw life.

It is in the words of Choctaw men and women living in the early twentieth century that the struggles over and the persistence of Choctaw cultural practices come through. Under the auspices of the Works Progress Administration in the 1930s, men and women were hired to interview Oklahoma citizens who had lived through the early history of the region. The records of those interviews make up the Indian Pioneer Papers Collection, and they encompass a wide variety of experiences, including those of the Choctaw. The interviewers asked about the past, and therefore many of the interviews consist of remembrances of former activities and practices. Many of them also contain references to ongoing practices, and those are the instances that provide insight into the maintenance of Choctaw culture.

Sarah Noah was born in 1889 in Oklahoma. Although she grew up during a time of great conflict for the Choctaw, it is clear that her relatives provided important information about Choctaw cultural practices. Through stories told around a warm fire in wintertime, her family transmitted important legacies of the Choctaw past. Her grandfather often told her stories about the bone-picking practices of their ancestors, and Sarah could remember in detail the activities he described. "The Choctaw Indians are great storytellers," she informed the man who interviewed her. And it was in part through such stories that the Choctaw culture continued.

Knowledge of the land and medical practices were also maintained into the 1930s and beyond. Jack Campbell was interviewed in the summer of 1937, when he was nearly 74 years old. A descendant of a slave mother and a Choctaw father,

Jack had learned the proper knowledge to become a doctor of traditional Choctaw medicine. At his advanced age, he did not practice full time but still visited sick American Indians if called to do so. Just as important, he refused to share more specific information regarding the roots and plants with his interviewer. "I never would tell the names of the roots and herbs that I dug up and cooked down for the sick," he explained. From his perspective, such cultural knowledge was both important and protected.

Verina Wesley Interview

In 1936, the University of Oklahoma and the Oklahoma State Historical Society received money from the federal government program known as the Works Progress Administration. The administration was formed to fund jobs for Americans during the Great Depression. The project in Oklahoma focused on conducting interviews with Oklahoma residents to record the early pioneer history of the territory and state.

As part of this project, more than 100 men and women conducted more than 11,000 interviews. Verina Wesley, who was born in the Choctaw Nation in August 1890, was interviewed as part of a Works Progress Administration project in 1937. The following excerpt from her interview provides some insight into the life of a Choctaw woman in the early twentieth century.

I was enrolled by the Dawes Commission at Talihina in 1898 or thereabouts, and then we made our filings on land in about 1903. We had to go to Atoka to file on our land, the land office being located there for the Choctaws. It took us several days to make the trip there and back.

The first payment the Choctaws had was in 1893, when they got $103.00 each. After that they did not get any

Evidence of cultural damage was also present in these interviews. Elba Gardner discussed the gradual loss of language. Like many Choctaw families of the late nineteenth and early twentieth centuries, Gardner's parents and grandparents tried to do what they believed was the best for the younger generations. As government schools and policies pushed for assimilation, some Choctaw decided it was best to cooperate. Elba's grandparents "would speak Choctaw when they didn't want the children to know what they were talking about, but would not teach it to

more payments for several years, then they got several payments.

We used to attend the Indian camp meeting; in fact, we used to camp at the church to help feed the people that came to attend the church. My father was an elder of the church during his lifetime, and we would go and camp with the other Choctaws every three months. This church is still in existence and is being used as the church yet. It was a Presbyterian church and named Wadesville Presbyterian church. Then we would attend another church which was called Post Oak Presbyterian church. This church was across the river from where we lived, about three miles from us. This church is an old church but it also is still there and being used by those Choctaws who are left.

I have attended the Indian cries. Some times they would have their cries at the church—but most of the time they would have them at the homes where the grave was located. Everyone there took part in the services and they would all get around the grave and cry, kinfolks or not. It is a very sad thing to attend one of those cries.

I never saw an Indian dance, nor a ball game. My mother and father were very devout Christians so they would not let us girls go to dances nor to a ball game, so I never did learn how to dance at all.

their children." Indeed, Elba's father only learned the language as an adult, and Elba did not learn it at all.

In the first several decades of the twentieth century, the federal government increased its efforts to undermine tribal cohesiveness and assimilate Indians into American society. But as the interviews of Choctaw in the 1930s revealed, those attempts did not always succeed in eliminating significant aspects of Choctaw identity. The strength and persistence of medical practices and storytelling laid important foundations for the continuities of cultural practices evidenced in the Choctaw Nation of Oklahoma today.

During World War I, the Choctaw men of the 36th Infantry Division were the first to use a Native American language as a military code. Pictured are members of the 36th Division's Company E (left to right): Solomon Lewis, Mitchell Bobb, James Edwards, Calvin Wilson, Joseph Davenport, and Captain E.H. Horner.

Choosing to remain Choctaw did not mean isolating themselves from the world around them. And crucial elements of Choctaw identity were put to great use on the global stage in the early twentieth century. During World War I, in fact, Choctaw soldiers played important roles because of their native language. The U.S. Army relied on Choctaw soldiers to transmit messages and orders that they did not want the enemy to understand. The Germans could not decipher any intercepted telephone communications because they did not know Choctaw. At least 14 Choctaw men served as what were later termed "code talkers" in World War I. Although the code talkers in World War II were largely Navajo men, more than 76 Choctaw men served in the American efforts against Germany and Japan.

THE CHOCTAW GOVERNMENT

Despite the heroic service of its citizens, the Choctaw Nation remained under assault. One of the foremost victims of federal policy from the late nineteenth to the late twentieth century was the Choctaw government. It was critical to the federal government's assimilation policy to remove the markers and structures that upheld tribal sovereignty. Yet the Choctaw government never completely disappeared. Even as legislation and policy aimed to remove Choctaw sovereignty, the Choctaw remained. By the 1970s, they had regained their status as a sovereign nation.

The Atoka Agreement of 1898 established a deadline for the eradication of the Choctaw national government. Although this led to a loss of power, it did not lead to elimination. The tribal government remained in place to oversee the final accounts of leases and land allotments. All of the problems associated with those dealings kept the Choctaw government around into the early 1950s. At that time, Harry Belvin was the appointed chief of the Choctaw. Belvin initiated a process to restore authority and sovereignty to the Choctaw.

Unfortunately, Belvin acted at a time when the federal government was making a substantial change in Indian affairs. Termination was enacted as a policy in 1953. The federal government hoped to "get out of the Indian business" by eliminating the special political and legal relationship it had with Indian tribes and nations. By dissolving, or terminating, the sovereign status of Indian governments, the government would accomplish that goal. When Belvin sought to initiate a new relationship with the federal government, his efforts led to the creation of termination legislation aimed specifically at the Choctaw in 1959. By the early 1960s, the Choctaw appeared to be on the verge of termination.

During the 1960s, however, Indian Country was as politically active and aware as any part of the United States. For the Choctaw, this meant that more men and women were aware of both federal and local politics. Choctaw citizens especially protested that Belvin had served for more than 20 years as a chief appointed by the federal government instead of being chosen by the Choctaw people. They also disliked that Belvin had managed to bring termination policy to the Choctaw. The Choctaw demanded the return of their political sovereignty as one more statement of their desire to maintain a Choctaw identity. As a result of their protests, in 1970, Congress officially repealed the legislation that would have ended the federal government's relationship with the Choctaw.

This victory led to a renewed effort to create a sovereign Choctaw government. Although it was not a simple process, in 1983, the Choctaw adopted a new constitution. This document spells out the geographic boundaries of the Choctaw Nation, requirements for membership, and voting rights. In addition to a bill of rights, the tribal constitution also contains a clear explanation of the executive, legislative, and judicial branches of the Choctaw government. Perhaps most importantly, the preamble states that the constitution is adopted "to secure to ourselves and our posterity the blessings of our ancestral heritage, culture and tribal sovereignty of the Choctaw Nation of Oklahoma."

The Choctaw government created under the 1983 constitution did not return to the Choctaw all the political power that had been lost over the course of the previous century. But it marked an important step in the resurgence of the Choctaw as a political entity in the late twentieth century.

At the beginning of the twentieth century, the Choctaw Nation approached the apparent end of its existence as a political entity. As the first decades of the 1900s unfolded, the land, economy, and culture of the Choctaw were under attack by a combination of public and private interests. Yet the Choctaw survived by asserting their right to be Choctaw and their pride in being Choctaw in all areas of life. Whether it was a protest against Oklahoma statehood or a willingness to serve in the military during wartime, Choctaw men and women did their best to engage with the world around them on their own terms. And as the twentieth century drew to a close, they had restored their government and retained the core of their cultural identity.

The Mississippi
Choctaw

Because the bulk of the Choctaw population moved west of the Mississippi River in the mid-nineteenth century, it is easy to forget that thousands remained behind. The Choctaw people who stayed in Mississippi under the terms of the Treaty of Dancing Rabbit Creek managed to survive in the midst of overwhelming circumstances. While spending most of the nineteenth and twentieth centuries on the margins of American life and history, the Mississippi Choctaw fought for land and federal recognition. Because of their persistence, they not only maintained and protected their community but also established a strong foundation in the state. By the end of the twentieth century, the Mississippi Choctaw had become a powerful cultural, economic, and political presence within the state of Mississippi.

PERSISTENCE IN MISSISSIPPI

The Treaty of Dancing Rabbit Creek, signed in 1830, arranged for the removal of the Choctaw from Mississippi. At the same time, the fourteenth article of that treaty stated that "each Choctaw head of a family being desirous to remain and become a citizen of the States, shall be permitted to do so." After the three government removals of the early 1830s, nearly 7,000 Choctaw remained in Mississippi. But any hope of taking advantage of the provisions of the fourteenth article was dashed by the efforts of Indian agent William Ward. Because of his unwillingness to assist the Choctaw and his determination to undermine the treaty terms, only 100 Choctaw registered for and received their land allotments.

Ward's willful negligence left the Choctaw in Mississippi without any territory or federal protection. Even those who had been able to register for allotments had difficulty holding on to those sections. A combination of sales, foreclosure, and fraud soon left most of the Mississippi Choctaw landless. When no assistance or follow-up arrived from the federal government, approximately 4,500 Choctaw left Mississippi and moved to Indian Territory in the mid-1840s. By the mid-1850s, only about 1,000 remained in the state. They did not have any land, and neither federal nor state governments granted them status as an American Indian tribe. These Choctaw men, women, and children survived by living on whatever they could find in the hills and swamps of the eastern-central region of the state.

Like their relatives in Oklahoma, the Mississippi Choctaw could not avoid the Civil War. They were residents of a secessionist state, and Choctaw men served in a number of different Confederate units during the four years of conflict. In an interesting twist, however, the Choctaw did not suffer any particular punishment at war's end. Because they were not a federally recognized tribe, the federal government ignored them and focused on the Mississippi state government. Like any other Mississippi resident, the Choctaw's postwar experience was defined by federal involvement at the state level and not at the individual level.

During the eighteenth century, the Choctaw were a prosperous people. After they were forced to give up their land to the federal government, the Choctaw quality of life greatly decreased. A 1918 U.S. Congress report described the tribe as "living in the poorest pocket of poverty in the poorest state in the country." Pictured is an example of reservation housing built by the U.S. government in the 1920s.

For the remainder of the nineteenth century, the Choctaw in Mississippi continued to find ways to make a living. Most of the Choctaw survived by farming as sharecroppers. They rented property from white landowners and paid their fees with the product of their harvest. It was an incredibly difficult existence, especially because most of the contracts in Mississippi made it difficult for the sharecropper to stay out of debt.

At the dawn of the twentieth century, most Choctaw were living in impoverished conditions. Although the federal government pushed for those in Mississippi to join their relatives in Oklahoma, not all did. As of 1910, therefore, 1,253 Choctaw still lived in Mississippi. Over the next decade, the population decreased by almost 150, primarily because of an influenza epidemic that hit the Choctaw particularly hard in 1918. The destitution of the Mississippi Choctaw reached a new low that year, and their condition brought a response at both the state and local level. A congressional investigation revealed that the average family income for the Choctaw was only one-fifth of the national average. These economic concerns were only one element, however. Most Choctaw lived without electricity or running water, and few had access to proper health care. Out of a population of approximately 1,100, fewer than 100 lived on land that they owned.

Finally, after nearly eight decades of negligence, the federal government decided it was necessary to aid the Choctaw living in Mississippi. The Bureau of Indian Affairs (BIA) was in charge of this assistance. The BIA was and is the office in the Department of the Interior that handles American Indian policy in the U.S. government. Its origins lie in the Office of Indian Affairs, first established in 1824. In its actions to help the Choctaw in the 1920s, the BIA first purchased land in the vicinity of the town of Philadelphia, Mississippi. In just over 10 years, nearly 18,000 acres (7,284 ha) of land had been purchased. It was held in trust by the federal government and distributed in 40-acre (16.2 ha) sections to Choctaw families and individuals. The BIA also built a hospital in Philadelphia to address the lack of adequate facilities for the Choctaw in the region. For the first time in more than a century, it appeared that the Mississippi Choctaw would have a measure of stability in their lives.

ROAD TO FEDERAL RECOGNITION

The intervention of the BIA in the lives of the Mississippi Choctaw occurred in the decade before federal government policy made a distinct and critical shift. Ever since the initiation of allotment policy, the federal government had focused its efforts on assimilating American Indians and breaking up tribal organizations. But in the early 1930s, a new commissioner of Indian Affairs named John Collier oversaw a complete turnaround. Collier's policies provided another important turning point for the Mississippi Choctaw. Within a matter of decades, they had taken steps to establish themselves as a federally recognized tribe.

The new political road opened to the Choctaw in 1934 when Congress passed the Wheeler-Howard Act, also known as the Indian Reorganization Act (IRA). Commissioner John Collier was the driving force behind this legislation. The main points of the IRA displayed a crucial change in American Indian affairs. Most importantly, the bill officially ended the policy of allotment and focused on reorganizing Indian tribes under new constitutions. Every Indian tribe in the country had the opportunity to take advantage of these terms if tribal members thought it would benefit them.

The Mississippi Choctaw moved quickly to adopt the IRA. A vote held in 1935 registered 218 in favor, 18 opposed, and 497 eligible voters who did not participate. The next step of the process involved drafting a constitution. It was not until 1945 that Secretary of the Interior Harold L. Ickes gave final approval for the Choctaw document. This approval came shortly after a December 1944 proclamation from the Department of the Interior that set aside more than 15,000 acres (6,070 ha) of land in Mississippi to be held in trust by the federal government for the Mississippi Choctaw. As of 1945, therefore, the Mississippi Band of Choctaw had obtained federal recognition and a central reservation in the state. The tribal council made up of 16 elected members met for the first time in July of that year. The transformation from landless and destitute to federal recognition and a reservation had taken fewer than three decades.

Although the Mississippi Choctaw had obtained federal recognition and adopted a constitution, these changes had not solved all of their problems. First, the new Choctaw government was not completely sovereign. In fact, reorganization under the IRA brought the Mississippi Choctaw under greater federal control.

Second, in 1974, a ruling by the Fifth District of the U.S. Court of Appeals delivered a potentially fatal blow to Indian sovereignty. This decision asserted that the Choctaw who stayed in Mississippi under the terms of the Treaty of Dancing Rabbit Creek had forever surrendered their rights as American Indians. According to this judgment, that choice had rendered meaningless any creation of a sovereign government or reservation in Mississippi. Fortunately for the Choctaw, the U.S. Supreme Court reversed that ruling. But the appeals court decision indicated that the struggle was not over. Third, and finally, the reservation land base did not automatically result in financial success for the entire community. As of 1964, in fact, approximately 90 percent of the Choctaw in Mississippi lived in poverty.

MISSISSIPPI CHOCTAW REVIVAL

Despite the problems still faced by the Mississippi Choctaw in the latter decades of the twentieth century, the work of the 1930s and 1940s had laid some very important foundations for success. The government formed under the IRA initially brought the Choctaw further under the control of the BIA. But it also established a platform for the growth of Choctaw authority. The rising influence of that Choctaw government and the individuals in that government also led to substantial economic improvements. By the end of the twentieth century, the Mississippi Band of Choctaw had become a model for economic development in Indian Country.

No single man or woman can be credited for all of the increased influence and effectiveness of the Mississippi Choctaw government over the latter decades of the 1900s. The tribal council has 16 members, and although there is an elected chairperson, all council members have worked to do their part. Nevertheless, it would be impossible to discuss the Choctaw government during this period without mentioning the impact of Phillip Martin. Martin first became an elected council member in 1957 and was elected chairman two years later. For the better part of the next

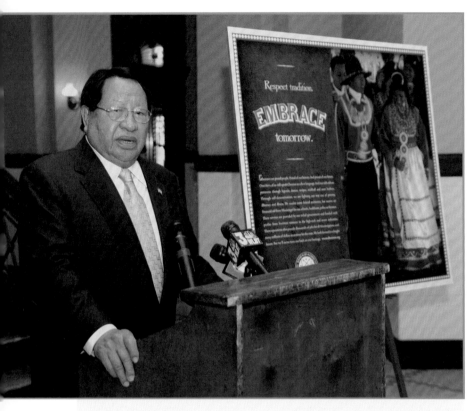

Before Phillip Martin's 23-year tenure as tribal chief of the Mississippi Band of Choctaw, his people faced limited possibilities, poor health conditions, and a substandard quality of life. In less than half a century, Martin's leadership and the tribe's hard work have made the Mississippi Choctaw into a highly skilled, self-reliant model of economic success whom companies seek to partner with today.

four decades, Martin was a nearly unstoppable force in Choctaw politics. A new constitution adopted in 1974 created separate legislative and executive branches and in the process created the position of chief. Martin was elected as chief in 1979 and served six consecutive four-year terms until 2007.

The increased effectiveness of the Choctaw government in general and Phillip Martin in particular coincided with economic developments. When Martin joined the tribal council in

Phillip Martin (1926–2010)

Phillip Martin was born on the Choctaw reservation in Tucker, Mississippi, in 1926. As a teenager, he left Mississippi to attend a boarding school in North Carolina for six years. At the age of 19, he left school and joined the Air Force. Martin served for approximately 10 years at American posts throughout the world. He returned to the Choctaw reservation in 1955 with his wife, Bonnie Kate Bell. The couple had two children, and while Bonnie Kate worked for the BIA agency, Phillip earned money through a series of jobs until he began to work for the Choctaw government full time in 1963.

Martin's service in the Choctaw government began in 1957 when he was first elected to the tribal council. Upon his reelection to the council in 1959, the other elected members chose him to be chairman. He held the position of chairman until 1966, when he resigned to lead the Choctaw Community Action Agency, a newly created organization in charge of distributing federal government assistance on the reservation. This period marked a five-year absence from tribal government for Martin. He returned to the position of chairman in 1971 and oversaw an important revision of the Choctaw Constitution. Under the auspices of this new constitution, Martin was elected chief of the Mississippi Band of Choctaw in 1979 and served six consecutive terms.

From 1957, when he first joined the Choctaw government, until 2007, Martin promoted and managed the economic revitalization of the Choctaw reservation in Mississippi. Under his leadership, the Mississippi Band of Choctaw became the third-largest employer in the state of Mississippi. Chief Martin died on February 4, 2010, at the age of 83.

the late 1950s, he had a particular vision for the governing body. Most importantly, he wanted to make the Choctaw government and its people less dependent on the federal government and its agencies. Martin strongly believed that the road to Choctaw self-determination would be built on economic independence. When the Choctaw had the ability to provide full financial support to their community, they would have the strength to fight for more political independence from the federal government.

This belief in economic development has served as the cornerstone for the Mississippi Choctaw government from the 1960s through the present. Because their reservation land was under the authority of a federally recognized tribe, the Choctaw had great advantages to offer private businesses. If the businesses built on tribal land, they would avoid state and local taxes and deal exclusively with a tribal government that wanted them to stay. Author Peter Ferrara quotes Phillip Martin in *The Choctaw Revolution* as having stated, "in our government, the Tribal Council is pro-business." This attitude would be increasingly attractive to a variety of national corporations in the decades that followed.

This economic plan had even greater importance for the Choctaw community at large. In the first half of the twentieth century, it was difficult to convince many young Choctaw men and women to stay in Mississippi. The reservation and surrounding towns did not have much to offer in the way of jobs. By bringing jobs to the reservation, however, the Choctaw government could now provide economic incentives to maintain and even build the population of their community. Phillip Martin actively recruited men and women who had taken up residence in other cities and states. As noted in the chronology section on the Mississippi Choctaw Web site, in 1983, Martin "traveled to Los Angeles, Chicago, and Cleveland to encourage the loose communities of Mississippi Choctaws to return to the reservation. He promised them jobs and economic opportunities."

Although it took some time for the economic foundation to grow, the business plan proved to be a success. In 1978, the Choctaw landed a huge deal when Packard Electric, a division of General Motors, chose to locate one of its plants on Choctaw lands. This contract also led to the formation of Chahta Enterprise, a Choctaw company that would handle the construction and operation of the plant. The next decade brought further development, but the 1990s witnessed one of the most critical economic additions. After Congress passed legislation in 1988 that allowed federally recognized tribes to operate casinos, the Mississippi Choctaw decided to act. In 1993, they broke ground on what became the Silver Star Hotel and Casino.

What is perhaps most important about the Silver Star Hotel and Casino is that it is only one of many successful operations managed by the Mississippi Choctaw. As a result, it is only one measure of economic success. Before the casino even opened, the Mississippi Choctaw businesses employed approximately 2,800 workers and brought in more than $90 million. Economic development did not focus solely on the casino after the mid-1990s. In other words, the Mississippi Band of Choctaw has a diverse economy in which the casino, while important, is one of many pieces.

This economic success has also had a widespread effect on Choctaw life in general. In 1975, for example, the average Choctaw had achieved a sixth-grade education. Fourteen years later, the average Choctaw had finished the eleventh grade. Economic independence even allowed the Choctaw government to assume full control of its school system, which had been managed by the Department of the Interior for nearly 70 years. With the creation of the Choctaw Tribal Scholarship Program, the Mississippi Band also guaranteed funding for college for tribal members. These efforts to assume control of the education of their children are powerful examples of the Mississippi Choctaw using their growing economic power to gain authority over critical aspects of their community's life.

The Choctaw have developed a diversified economy that includes manufacturing, retail, service, and government jobs. The revenue from these businesses has enabled the tribe to finance college educations, build schools and day care centers, and build up its social and health care services. Pictured is the Silver Star Resort and Casino, Mississippi's only land-based casino and highest-grossing gambling operation.

MISSISSIPPI CHOCTAW COMMUNITY

Any description of the rise of the economic and political power of the Mississippi Band of Choctaw in the twentieth century can be somewhat misleading. It paints a picture of the ways in which economics and politics helped to stabilize and save the Mississippi Choctaw. Yet it is crucial to recognize that the strongest foundation of the Choctaw community in Mississippi has always been and remains the people and the distinctive culture they maintain, protect, and cherish. The language, artwork, and other traditions that Choctaw men, women, and children continue to uphold survived the suffering of the nineteenth and early twentieth centuries. Although the importance of the economic revival to Choctaw culture should not be downplayed, its impact should also not be overstated.

A scholar named Tom Mould first visited the Mississippi Choctaw in 1995. Over the next decade and more, he spent hours visiting with Choctaw men and women and recorded many of their stories. The book he published from those conversations focused on the tales and histories that had been passed down over generations. This collection in and of itself is a testament to the ways in which the individual Choctaw men and women represent the continued strength of the Mississippi Band of Choctaw.

All of the stories Mould recorded are important markers of both the traditional roots and ongoing vitality of the Mississippi Choctaw. His book includes what Mould labels creation stories, supernatural legends, animal stories, prophecy, and other genres. Terry Ben, a Choctaw man living in Pearl River, Mississippi, told Mould a brief story about the origin of corn, and Odie Mae Anderson, a Choctaw woman from Conehatta, Mississippi, spoke to him about the story of lightning and thunder. Ben and Anderson are not simply spinning tales. As Mould notes in his introduction to *Choctaw Tales*, "Stories of origin and creation are important, not only because they serve as reminders of a communal past, but because they reflect upon the views and values of the present." The Mississippi Choctaw have endured numerous changes over the past two centuries, and these stories have both grounded them and changed with them.

The last section of *Choctaw Tales* encompasses 16 different stories, all recorded and printed in the Choctaw language. Perhaps this is the best evidence of Mississippi Choctaw perseverance and strength. Language is more than words put together in a certain order. Linguistic expression is a central pillar of culture, and the presentation of Choctaw histories, tales, and legends in the Choctaw language is a clear reminder of that fact. Despite the passage of time and all of the changes that have occurred, the Mississippi Band is a strong and successful community. But above all else, they are and will remain Choctaw.

The Choctaw have never really left Mississippi. It is true that the Treaty of Dancing Rabbit Creek and the government removals of the early 1830s relocated thousands of Choctaw from their homeland. However, the continued presence and growth of the Mississippi Band of Choctaw in the present illustrate the enduring cultural and communal strength that has enabled them to keep Mississippi as part of Choctaw Country.

The Choctaw in the Twenty-first Century

At the end of the first decade of the twenty-first century, the situation for the Choctaw looks stronger than it has in years. There are at present three federally recognized Choctaw tribes in the United States. The Choctaw Nation of Oklahoma is the largest, followed in size by the Mississippi Band of Choctaw and the Jena Band of Choctaw in Louisiana. While the three communities live as distinct entities, they all share a common legacy in the foundations of Choctaw history. Their experiences of the past continue to shape their lives in the present.

CHOCTAW LIVES

The word *Oklahoma* is of Choctaw origin. *Okla* means "people," and *houmma* is the Choctaw word for "red." Yet, as of 2006, of the nearly 175,000 enrolled members of the Choctaw Nation of Oklahoma, most lived outside of that state. Only 29,000 Choctaw men, women, and children live in a 10-county area that encompasses a fraction of the acreage once secured to the Choctaw by the Treaty of Doak's Stand. The tribal government that oversees this population also manages a sizable budget of around $300 million and manages a multitude of business operations. Like their relatives in Mississippi, the Choctaw Nation has created a strong economic foundation through diverse economic development that includes casino gaming. Similar to the Mississippi Band of Choctaw, the Choctaw Nation of Oklahoma has also achieved a measure of financial self-sufficiency.

At present, the Mississippi Band of Choctaw has an enrolled membership of nearly 10,000. In a critical measure of the community's future, half of the population is under the age of 25. Although the tough economic times at the end of the first decade of the twenty-first century slowed the economic growth of Choctaw operations, the tribe continues to have a tremendous financial impact on the state of Mississippi. Indeed, some estimates place the tribe's economic influence at more than $1 billion annually. In addition, one look at the tribal publication *Choctaw Community News* illustrates the strong community centered on the Choctaw reservation lands totaling 35,000 acres (14,164 ha) located throughout Mississippi.

The Jena Band of Choctaw gained federal recognition in 1995. The present community of nearly 250 is descended from the members of five families who settled in Louisiana even as their relatives moved farther west during the removal era. A small but strong community persisted throughout the nineteenth and twentieth centuries until its members gained recognition from both state and federal governments. They were landless in 1995 but now maintain a small reservation in LaSalle Parish in northern Louisiana about 50 miles (80 km) west of the Mississippi River.

All three Choctaw communities maintain a strong presence in the modern world with official Web sites. In these online forums, communities both present information about their government and tell the history of their people. It is one more way in which the Choctaw are able to maintain connections within a population that is spread throughout the country. The use of these Web sites also provides a crucial forum for informing the American public about who the Choctaw are, where they have been, and what they are doing.

CHOCTAW CHALLENGES

The Choctaw of Oklahoma, Mississippi, and Louisiana continue to face substantial tests in the twenty-first century. The most prominent challenge is the ongoing protection and preservation of tribal sovereignty. This struggle has two dimensions. First, the Choctaw have to defend against attacks made in the legal arena. Like American Indian nations throughout the country, they have continually found it necessary to assert and protect their treaty rights. One court case finally resolved in the early twenty-first century involved the boundaries of Choctaw lands established by treaties in the 1800s. The Choctaw, along with the Cherokee and Chickasaw, went to court for damages created by the federal government's mismanagement of land that belonged to the tribes. Although the U.S. Supreme Court had ruled in favor of the tribes in the case of *Choctaw Nation v. Oklahoma*, it took more than three decades for a final resolution. Congress finally passed what was known as the Arkansas River Bed Settlement in 2003.

A second factor in the struggle over sovereignty revolves around education and public relations. The Choctaw need to educate the American public about the nature of the government-to-government relationship established through treaties. Indian sovereignty may be one of the least understood—or most misunderstood—aspects of American history. Events of the past several decades have only complicated matters. The financial achievements of the Choctaw in Oklahoma and Mississippi are often used as examples to support the elimination of tribal sovereignty. It is often argued that Indian economic self-sufficiency

In November 1997, Chief Phillip Martin (*seated, right*) and Mississippi Governor Kirk Fordice (*seated, left*) signed the first-ever pact between their two governments, recognizing the sovereign nature of the Choctaw government and promising a spirit of cooperation and respect. Fordice's chief of staff, Mark Garriga, and Tribal Secretary Treasurer Hayward Bell witnessed their signing.

should result in the end of so-called special treatment for Indians. Such misunderstandings are one of the reasons behind the Choctaw's active engagement with such discussions. In 1997, for example, Chief Phillip Martin signed an agreement with then Mississippi Governor Kirk Fordice that acknowledged the importance of respecting and nurturing the government-to-government relationship between the tribe and the state.

A second potential challenge is connected to the issue of sovereignty but focuses more on citizenship. It is also one of the controversial legacies of the Choctaw past that involves primarily the Choctaw Nation of Oklahoma and the descendants of former slaves. The Treaty of 1866 officially ended slavery among the Choctaw and stated that the freedmen should become members of the tribe. Yet it was not until 1885 that the freedmen received their designated rights as Choctaw citizens. Over the course of the nineteenth and twentieth centuries, the lives of the Choctaw and freedmen became intertwined in a number of ways. Most recently, however, in the constitution adopted by the Choctaw Nation of Oklahoma in 1983, membership was based on blood descent from an individual listed on the Dawes Commission rolls. In sum, this new constitution denied citizenship to the descendants of freedmen.

The Choctaw are not alone in this controversy over tribal citizenship. In 2007, the Cherokee Nation of Oklahoma voted to deny citizenship to freedmen and their descendants. Both the Creek and Chickasaw also deny citizenship to the descendants of freedmen. On the one hand, the actions taken by these four communities is an assertion of their respective rights as sovereign nations. They have the power to determine the criteria for membership. American Indian nations believe it is critical to maintain and protect that right as an illustration of sovereignty. On the other hand, the positions taken by the Choctaw and others have been criticized as a strictly racial decision by groups throughout the United States. Active political groups like Descendants of Freedmen of the Five Civilized Tribes and Choctaw and Chickasaw Freedmen Descendants of Oklahoma continue to protest the recent Cherokee vote and the Choctaw membership criteria.

Last, but certainly not least, among the challenges faced by the Choctaw in the twenty-first century is the general health and welfare of their far-reaching community. In Mississippi, Louisiana, and Oklahoma, the Choctaw governments have made vast strides in improving the access to and quality of health care. They have also put a tremendous amount of effort into creating a strong educational system. But the health and strength of the community also depends on the ongoing preservation and renewal of Choctaw culture and identity. Events like the annual Choctaw Indian Fair in Mississippi are small pieces of a larger struggle to maintain the practices and customs of the past. But the Choctaw in Oklahoma and Mississippi are also working hard to regain what has been lost and taken. Efforts to keep the Choctaw language alive represent a substantial piece of that battle.

CHOCTAW HISTORIES

The effort to preserve the Choctaw culture includes historical accounts. Choctaw scholar D.L. Birchfield has written, "No one has ever published a satisfactory synthesis of all of Choctaw history." This is most certainly true. In his book, *How Choctaws Invented*

Due to economic success, job opportunities, and an educational structure that prepares tribal members for jobs, young Choctaw have chosen to stay in tribal communities. Today, their children and grandchildren can choose their own fate and benefit from the tribe's accomplishments. Above, Choctaw dancers perform a traditional blessing dance during the grand opening of the Choctaw Casino in Grant, Oklahoma, in 2005.

Planes, Roads, and Culture

Grady John was a Choctaw man who lived in Henning, Tennessee. John was best known for his work as a Choctaw potter. In 1998, Grady John told the following story to Tom Mould.

You know, my grandpa predicted lot of things I didn't believe but that's happened.

He said, "You see that bird?"—one time I was a small kid—"We going to see, like that, going to be flying over you."

"And *hinakta sa losa*?" He said, "That's blacktop. It's going to be all over. People driving the car, he's going to see car, people be driving. You're going to hear the wagon, you're going to put it away. These things going to change."

One day, he picked one time: "The tractor. You ain't going to use—to find anymore like that horse."

I didn't believe him. "Ah, quit telling me that Grandpa," you know? I thought I knew it all at ten years old. I didn't know a thing. I'd rather listen to my granddad now.

But, you know, he predict something.

He said, "All these schools, there are going to be bunch of new schools. You know what? They're going to study about you. You better keep your blowguns, you better keep your things. You can be sure then. That's how it's going to be—education."

And it's true.

I used to sit there and think, "Grandpa, what do you know?"

And he'd say, "Grady, you're going to find out. It'll be too late then."

"Don't be ashamed to wear your shirt." He said, "Choctaw shirt—wear that when you go to the Choctaw Fair. You're a Choctaw. Be proud of what you are."

That's what he used to say.

Civilization and Why Choctaws Will Conquer the World, Birchfield demonstrates the need for such a synthesis. His book confronts head on the idea that American history and historians have done the Choctaw and others a grave injustice. Choctaw history, from his perspective, has been misrepresented and misinformed for far too long in the service of a larger narrative of American history. Birchfield also asserts without hesitation or apology that the Choctaw "are not merely different from other Native peoples of North America, but they are markedly distinctive from any other people on earth, and they have a fundamental right to remain different."

How the Choctaws Invented Civilization is an important book for a number of reasons. First and foremost, it is a book that forces the reader to ask questions about how history, and American Indian history in particular, is written and taught within the United States. Whether or not a reader agrees or disagrees with some of Birchfield's statements is less important than the fact that his writing demands the reader ask questions about representations of the past. Second, and just as important, the book provides a Choctaw point of view on Choctaw history.

The Choctaw have always maintained and protected their history and culture. Tom Mould's collections of tales, legends, and stories from the Mississippi Choctaw are perfect illustrations of that fact. Even as outsiders from the eighteenth century to the present have written essays, articles, and books about the Choctaw experience, Choctaw men and women have retained a hold on the histories that ground their families, communities, and culture. They are stories that have allowed the Choctaw to endure all of the changes over the past three centuries without losing the core of what it means to be Choctaw.

Change has not diminished the Choctaw. As Clara Sue Kidwell states in the last sentence of her book, *The Choctaw in Oklahoma*, the adaptability of the Choctaw Nation "has and will sustain it in the future." She refers to the political and legal adaptations of the Choctaw as a communal entity, but her statement also describes the adaptations of individuals. Indeed, Clara Sue Kidwell is perhaps the most prominent of what has become over the last several decades a host of Choctaw scholars and artists who have taken on the project of examining and presenting the Choctaw experience. Devon Mihesuah's new book, *Choctaw Crime and Punishment*, looks at developments in the Choctaw Nation of Oklahoma in the late nineteenth and early twentieth centuries. Michelene E. Pesantubbee is another historian whose book, *Choctaw Women in a Chaotic World*, provides a critical look at the place and role of women in the history of Euro-American–Choctaw relations. Those scholars are only two of a long list of Choctaw men and women writing, painting, and examining the Choctaw past, present, and future.

Birchfield writes that "there are, and always have been, quite a variety of different kinds of Choctaws." Any history of the Choctaw, therefore, can hardly account for all of the people and the experiences of the past and the present. It can be said, however, that the Choctaw of the twenty-first century, whether they live in Mississippi, Louisiana, or Oklahoma, off or on reservation lands, are in some manner a product of the history described in this book. In short, the Choctaw past informs and influences the Choctaw present. And it is the actions and the stories of the Choctaw men and women in the past that have helped create the opportunities for the Choctaw men and women in the present.

Chronology

1539–1542 Hernando de Soto expedition travels through the Southeast and encounters villages and peoples of the Mississippian civilizations.

1699 French expedition led by Pierre Le Moyne d'Iberville encounters members of Choctaw confederacy.

1746–1750 The Choctaw Civil War occurs as Choctaw villages allied with the British and the French attack each other.

Timeline

1699

French expedition led by Pierre Le Moyne d'Iberville encounters members of the Choctaw confederacy

1786

The Choctaw sign Hopewell Treaty, the first treaty signed between the Choctaw and the United States

1830

In May, Congress passes the Indian Removal Act

1650 **1800**

1746–1750

The Choctaw Civil War occurs as Choctaw villages allied with the British and the French attack each other

1820

The Choctaw sign Treaty of Doak's Stand that cedes 5 million acres of land in Mississippi.

1831–1833

Three stages of Choctaw removal from Mississippi

1763	The Seven Years' War ends, and the French surrender all claims to territory in North America east of the Mississippi.
1786	The Choctaw sign the Hopewell Treaty, the first treaty signed between the Choctaw and the United States.
1817	Mississippi becomes the twentieth state in the Union.
1820	Choctaw sign Treaty of Doak's Stand, which cedes 5 million acres (2 million ha) of land in Mississippi.
1830	In May, Congress passes the Indian Removal Act.
1830	In September, Choctaw delegates sign Treaty of Dancing Rabbit Creek that arranges for the tribe's removal west of the Mississippi River.
1831–1833	The three stages of Choctaw removal from Mississippi.
1834	The Intercourse Act of 1834 officially creates Indian Territory, which is all American territory west of the

1861

Choctaw leaders sign a treaty with the Confederate States of America and agree to fight against the Union

1907

Oklahoma becomes the forty-sixth state in the Union and brings the Choctaw in Indian Territory under the new state's government

1983

Choctaw Nation of Oklahoma adopts a new constitution that establishes rules for membership and political structure

1900 — 1995

1834

The Intercourse Act of 1834 officially creates Indian Territory

1896

U.S. Congress forms the Dawes Commission; two years later, the Atoka Agreement imposes allotment on Choctaw in Indian Territory

1995

Jena Band of Choctaw obtains federal recognition

	Mississippi River not included in Missouri, Louisiana, or Arkansas.
1861	Choctaw leaders in Indian territory sign a treaty with the Confederate States of America and agree to fight against the Union.
1866	The Choctaw in Indian territory sign the Treaty of 1866 at the end of the Civil War to reestablish peaceful relations with the United States.
1871	The Choctaw in Indian Territory sign the Okmulgee Constitution, which expresses their support for Indian autonomy in the region.
1887	The U.S. Congress passes the General Allotment Act, also known as the Dawes Act, which intends to divide up Indian lands and make Indians farmers and private landowners.
1896	The U.S. Congress forms the Dawes Commission with the intention of imposing allotment on the Five Civilized Tribes of Indian Territory.
1898	The Atoka Agreement imposes allotment on the Choctaw in Indian Territory.
1902	The Choctaw in Indian territory sign the Supplementary Agreement that sets restrictions on land distributed through allotment.
1907	Oklahoma becomes the forty-sixth state in the Union and brings the Choctaw in Indian Territory under the new state's government.
1934	The U.S. Congress passes the Indian Reorganization Act.
1945	The constitution of the Mississippi Band of Choctaw written under the terms of the Indian Reorganization Act is approved by the Department of the Interior.
1983	The Choctaw Nation of Oklahoma adopts a new constitution that establishes rules for membership and political structure.
1995	The Jena Band of Choctaw obtains federal recognition.

Glossary

Allotment A U.S. government policy from the 1880s to the 1920s in which Indian lands were divided up and distributed to individual men and women in an effort to turn Indians into farmers.

Atoka Agreement An agreement signed by the Choctaw in 1898 that arranged for the allotment of Choctaw lands and an end to the Choctaw government.

Bureau of Indian Affairs The office of the U.S. government in the Department of the Interior that is in charge of Indian affairs; it was known as the Office of Indian Affairs when established in 1824.

charnel house A structure in which human skeletal remains are stored.

confederacy A political alliance of individuals or communities formed out of mutual interest.

fanimingo An individual who played an important role in inter-Indian diplomacy and advocated for his adopted tribe in times of war.

federal recognition A status that creates a government-to-government relationship between an Indian tribe and the U.S. government.

General Allotment Act Also known as the Dawes Act, the legislation passed by Congress in 1887 that established the allotment policy.

iksa A term for clans that comprised the Imoklasha and Inhulahta ethnic divisions.

Imoklasha One of two ethnic divisions among the Choctaw.

Indian Removal Act Legislation passed by Congress in 1830 that authorized the president to negotiate for the purchase of Indian lands east of the Mississippi River in exchange for territory west of the Mississippi River.

Indian Territory American territory located west of the Mississippi River not included in Missouri, Louisiana, or Arkansas and intended to be home to Indians removed from eastern lands.

Inhulahta   One of two ethnic divisions among the Choctaw; considered to be the elder brothers of the Imoklasha.

maize   Name for corn, the crop that was the foundation of Choctaw agriculture and subsistence.

Nanih Waiya   The sacred mound that is the site of Choctaw origin; located near Philadelphia, Mississippi.

Okmulgee Constitution   An agreement among the tribes of Indian Territory in 1871 expressing their resistance to the creation of a state out of Indian Territory.

secede/secession   Terms that have to do with leaving; a reference to the Southern states that left the Union after Lincoln's election to form their own country.

sovereign/sovereignty   Political terms that reference independence and autonomy; a sovereign nation is an independent nation.

Termination   A U.S. government policy in the 1950s and 1960s that attempted to end the federal economic and political ties to Indian tribes and nations.

Treaty of 1866   An agreement signed by the Choctaw in Indian territory with the U.S. government at the end of the Civil War that reestablished peaceful relations between the United States and the Choctaw.

Treaty of Dancing Rabbit Creek   An agreement signed by the Choctaw in 1830 with the U.S. government that surrendered their land in Mississippi and arranged for their removal west of the Mississippi River.

Treaty of Doak's Stand   An agreement signed by the Choctaw in 1820 with the U.S. government that surrendered 5 million acres (2 million ha) of land in Mississippi in exchange for approximately 15 million acres (6 million ha) of land west of the Mississippi River.

Treaty of Hopewell   An agreement signed by the Choctaw in 1786 with the U.S. government that intended to establish peaceful relations.

Treaty of San Lorenzo   An agreement signed in 1795 between Spain and the United States that recognized boundaries between Spanish and American territory and opened the Mississippi River to American trade.

Bibliography

Akers, Donna L. *Living in the Land of Death: The Choctaw Nation, 1830–1860.* East Lansing: Michigan State University Press, 2004.

"An Interview with Mrs. Verina Wesley," Indian Pioneer Paper Collection, Volume 96, University of Oklahoma. Available online. URL: http://digital.libraries.ou.edu/whc/pioneer/paper.asp?pID=6500&vID=96.

Baird, W. David. *Peter Pitchlynn: Chief of the Choctaws.* Norman: University of Oklahoma Press, 1972.

Birchfield, D.L. *How Choctaws Invented Civilization and Why Choctaws Will Conquer the World.* Albuquerque: University of New Mexico Press, 2007.

Carson, James Taylor. *Searching for the Bright Path: The Mississippi Choctaws from Prehistory to Removal.* Lincoln: University of Nebraska Press, 1999.

Catlin, George. *Letters and Notes on the Manners, Customs, and Conditions of North American Indians.* 2 vols. New York: Dover Publications, 1973.

Debo, Angie. *The Rise and Fall of the Choctaw Republic.* Norman: University of Oklahoma Press, 1934.

DeRosier Jr., Arthur H. *The Removal of the Choctaw Indians.* Knoxville: University of Tennessee Press, 1970.

Ferrara, Peter J. *The Choctaw Revolution: Lessons for Federal Indian Policy.* Washington, D.C.: Americans for Tax Reform Foundation, 1998.

Galloway, Patricia. *Choctaw Genesis, 1500–1700.* Lincoln: University of Nebraska Press, 1995.

———. *Practicing Ethnohistory: Mining Archives, Hearing Testimony, Constructing Narrative.* Lincoln: University of Nebraska Press, 2006.

Howe, LeAnne. *Shell Shaker.* San Francisco, Calif.: Aunt Lute Books, 2001.

Kehoe, Alice B. *North American Indians: A Comprehensive Account.* 3rd ed. Upper Saddle River, N.J.: Prentice Hall, 2006.

Kidwell, Clara Sue. *Choctaws and Missionaries in Mississippi, 1818–1918.* Norman: University of Oklahoma Press, 1995.

———. *The Choctaws in Oklahoma: From Tribe to Nation, 1855–1970.* Norman: University of Oklahoma Press, 2007.

Lambert, Valerie. "Political Protest, Conflict, and Tribal Nationalism: The Oklahoma Choctaws and the Termination Crisis of 1959–1970." *American Indian Quarterly* 31:2 (Spring 2007): 283–309.

Lowrie, Walter, and Matthew St. Clair Clarke, eds., *American State Papers, Documents, Legislative and Executive, of the Congress of the United States (1789–1815), Class II, Indian Affairs.* Washington, D.C.: Gales and Seaton, 1832.

McKee, Jesse O., and Jon A. Schlenker. *The Choctaws: Cultural Evolution of a Native American Tribe.* Jackson: University Press of Mississippi, 1980.

Mould, Tom, ed. *Choctaw Tales.* Jackson: University Press of Mississippi, 2004.

O'Brien, Greg. "Protecting Trade Through War: Choctaw Elites and British Occupation of the Floridas." In *Empire and Others: British Encounters with Indigenous Peoples, 1600–1850,* edited by Martin Daunton and Rick Halper. Philadelphia: University of Pennsylvania Press, 1999.

———. *Choctaws in a Revolutionary Age, 1750–1830.* Lincoln: University of Nebraska Press, 2002.

———, ed. *Pre-Removal Choctaw History: Exploring New Paths.* Norman: University of Oklahoma Press, 2008.

Pesantubbee, Michelene E. *Choctaw Women in a Chaotic World: The Clash of Cultures in the Colonial Southeast.* Albuquerque: University of New Mexico Press, 2005.

Reeves, Carolyn Keller, ed. *The Choctaw Before Removal.* Jackson: University Press of Mississippi, 1985.

Rowland, Dunbar, ed. *Mississippi Provincial Archives: English Dominion.* Nashville, Tenn.: Press of Brandon, 1911.

Swanton, John R. *Source Material for the Social and Ceremonial Life of the Choctaw Indians.* Bureau of American Ethnology Bulletin 103. Washington, D.C.: Government Printing Office, 1931.

Usner Jr., Daniel H. *Indians, Settlers, and Slaves in a Frontier Exchange Economy: The Lower Mississippi Valley Before 1783.* Chapel Hill: University of North Carolina Press, 1992.

White, Richard. *The Roots of Dependency: Subsistence, Environment, and Social Change Among the Choctaws, Pawnees, and Navajos.* Lincoln: University of Nebraska Press, 1983.

Young, Mary Elizabeth. *Redskins, Ruffleshirts, and Rednecks: Indian Allotments in Alabama and Mississippi.* Norman: University of Oklahoma Press, 1961.

Further Resources

Cushman, H.B. *History of the Choctaw, Chickasaw and Natchez Indians.* Rev. ed. Edited by Angie Debo. Norman: University of Oklahoma Press, 1999.

Lambert, Valerie. *Choctaw Nation: A Story of American Indian Resurgence.* Lincoln: University of Nebraska Press, 2007.

Mihesuah, Devon Abbott. *Choctaw Crime and Punishment, 1884–1907.* Norman: University of Oklahoma Press, 2009.

Mould, Tom. *Choctaw Prophecy: A Legacy of the Future.* Tuscaloosa: University of Alabama Press, 2003.

Web Sites

Choctaw Nation of Oklahoma
http://www.choctawnation.com
This Web site was created by the Choctaw Nation of Oklahoma to provide information to tribal members and others who want to know more about the Choctaw. There are links to information about the tribe's government, programs, culture, and history.

Indian Arts and Crafts Board (IACB)
http://www.iacb.doi.gov/museums/general_museum.html
This agency within the U.S. Department of the Interior promotes the economic development of American Indians and Alaska Natives through the Indian arts and crafts market. The IACB operates three regional museums: the Sioux Indian Museum in Rapid City, South Dakota; the Museum of the Plains Indians in Browning, Montana; and the Southern Plains Indian Museum in Anadarko, Oklahoma.

Jena Band of Choctaw Indians
http://www.jenachoctaw.org
This Web site was created by the Jena Band to provide information to tribal members and others who want to know more about their particular

history. In addition, it provides information about the tribe's mission statement and current issues.

Mississippi Band of Choctaw Indians
http://www.choctaw.org/index.htm
This Web site was created by the Mississippi Band to provide information to tribal members and others who want to know more about the Choctaw. It includes links to information about the tribe's government, economy, culture, and history.

Museum of the Red River
http://www.museumoftheredriver.org/index.html
This museum, located in Idabel, Oklahoma, houses artifacts dating back 10,000 years from Oklahoma, Texas, and Arkansas. The Web site also features a Choctaw history and chronology, photos of items from the museum's collections, and a calendar of events of its upcoming programs and activities.

Picture Credits

PAGE:

18: © Michael S. Lewis / CORBIS

21: © Infobase Publishing

25: © North Wind / Nancy Carter / North Wind Picture Archives—
     All rights reserved.

30: © North Wind Picture Archives / Alamy

36: © Infobase Publishing

43: © North Wind Picture Archives / Alamy

48: © North Wind Picture Archives / Alamy

52: English School / The Bridgeman Art Library/Getty Images

57: Photo by MPI / hulton Archive / Getty Images

65: © Infobase Publishing

66: Agreement documenting the forced removal of the Indians from
     their homeland in Georgia, 24th April 1831 (litho), American School,
     (19th century) / Private Collection / Peter Newark American Pictures /
     The Bridgeman Art Library

71: Smithsonian American Art Museum, Washington, DC /
     Art Resource, NY

74: Smithsonian American Art Museum, Washington, DC /
     Art Resource, NY

79: Railroad Building on the Great Plains, from 'Harper's Weekly', 17th July
     1875 (etching), Waud, Alfred R. (1828–91) (after) / Newberry Library,
     Chicago, Illinois, USA / The Bridgeman Art Library International

84: © Infobase Publishing

88: ELIOT KAMENITZ / The Times-Picayune / Landov

92: RODGER MALLISON / MCT / Landov

98: © Ed Kashi / Corbis

102: Kyle Carter / he Neshoba Democrat / AP Photo

106: Rogelio Solis / AP Photo

112: Rogelio Solis / AP Photo

114: Sam Craft / The Paris News / AP Photo

Index

About the Contributors

Author **JOHN P. BOWES** is an assistant professor of Native American history at Eastern Kentucky University. Cambridge University Press published his first book, *Exiles and Pioneers: Eastern Indians in the Trans-Mississippi West*, as a part of its series Studies in North American Indian History. Dr. Bowes has also written two books for Chelsea House in its Landmark Events in Native American History series. Those two books are titled *The Trail of Tears: Removal in the South* and *Black Hawk and the War of 1832: Removal in the North*.

Series editor **PAUL C. ROSIER** received his Ph.D. in American history from the University of Rochester in 1998. Dr. Rosier currently serves as associate professor of history at Villanova University (Villanova, Pennsylvania), where he teaches Native American History, American Environmental History, Global Environmental Justice Movements, History of American Capitalism, and World History.

In 2001 the University of Nebraska Press published his first book, *Rebirth of the Blackfeet Nation, 1912–1954*; in 2003, Greenwood Press published *Native American Issues* as part of its Contemporary Ethnic American Issues series. In 2006, he co-edited an international volume called *Echoes from the Poisoned Well: Global Memories of Environmental Injustice*. Dr. Rosier has also published articles in the *American Indian Culture and Research Journal*, the *Journal of American Ethnic History*, and *The Journal of American History*. His *Journal of American History* article, titled "They Are Ancestral Homelands: Race, Place, and Politics in Cold War Native America, 1945–1961," was selected for inclusion in *The Ten Best History Essays of 2006–2007*, published by Palgrave MacMillan in 2008; and it won the Western History Association's 2007 Arrell Gibson Award for Best Essay on the history of Native Americans. In 2009, Harvard University Press published his latest book, *Serving Their Country: American Indian Politics and Patriotism in the Twentieth Century*.